Mestizo in America

Mestizo in America

Generations of Mexican Ethnicity in the Suburban Southwest

Thomas Macias

The University of Arizona Press   Tucson

The University of Arizona Press
© 2006 Arizona Board of Regents
All rights reserved
This book is printed on acid-free, archival-quality paper.
Manufactured in the United States of America

11 10 09 08 07 06 6 5 4 3 2 1

Library of Congress Cataloging-in-Publication Data
Macias, Thomas, 1967–
    Mestizo in America : generations of Mexican ethnicity in
the suburban Southwest / Thomas Macias.
        p. cm.
    Includes bibliographical references and index.
    ISBN-13: 978-0-8165-2504-1 (hardcover : alk. paper)
    ISBN-10: 0-8165-2504-8 (hardcover : alk. paper)
    ISBN-13: 978-0-8165-2505-8 (pbk. : alk. paper)
    ISBN-10: 0-8165-2505-6 (pbk. : alk. paper)
    1. Mexican Americans—Southwest, New—Social conditions.
    2. Mexican Americans—Southwest, New—Ethnic identity.
    3. Mexican Americans—Southwest, New—Interviews.
    4. Mestizos—Southwest, New—Social conditions. 5. Immigrants
    —Southwest, New—Social conditions. 6. Social integration—
    Southwest, New. 7. Phoenix (Ariz.)—Ethnic relations. 8. San
    Jose (Calif.)—Ethnic relations. 9. Interviews—Arizona—Phoenix.
    10. Interviews—California—San Jose. I. Title.
    F790.M5 M47 2006
    305.868'72073079—dc22
                                                2006005716

I dedicate this book to the memory of my father, Joe Macias.

Contents

List of Illustrations   ix

Preface: A Mestizo Point of View   xi

Acknowledgments   xv

1 The Restricted Entry of a Forbidden Term   3

2 Imagining Mexican American Culture   25

3 Work, Organizations, and the Legacy of Chicanismo   44

4 The Social Contours of American Mestizaje   67

5 Mexican-Origin Identities Past the Second Generation   94

6 Imagining Mestizaje in a Sociological Way   116

Appendix I. Selected Respondent Attributes   134

Appendix II. Third-Plus-Generation Mexican American Interview Schedule   139

Appendix III. Sample Selection and Interview Procedures   143

Appendix IV. Methodological Appendix for Chapter 4   145

Notes   149

Bibliography   157

Index   167

Illustrations

Figures

4.1 Predicted probabilities of intermarriage by independent variables   89

A.1 Question #5 from the 2000 census   139

Tables

4.1 Estimated Size of Latino Population   69

4.2 Selected Characteristics of Mexican Americans   71

4.3 Educational Attainment Percentages   73

4.4 Occupational Status Percentages   73

4.5 Family Household Income Percentages   74

4.6 Mexican-origin Intermarriage Percentages   77

4.7 Percentages of Mexican-origin/Anglo Intermarriage   78

4.8 Percentages or Means in the Mexican-origin Population for Selected Variables   85

4.9 Estimated Coefficients of Selected Logistic Regression Models of Mexican American Intermarriage with Anglos   87

6.1 Structural Determinants of American Mestizaje   123

Selected Respondent Attributes   134

Preface

A Mestizo Point of View

One of the most striking memories I have from childhood is going to a federal office in downtown Phoenix with my father to get my social security card. I must have been about age ten, ready to take on my first job as a newspaper delivery boy. My relative financial independence was palpable, and my dad reinforced this theme by letting me fill out the half-page government application myself. All was fine until I came to the late-1970s version of the race question. Let's see, there was white, black, Asian, Indian, and Other. The Hispanic ethnic option was not there. Not seeing a box labeled "Mexican"—the way we thought of ourselves at home and the way I thought about myself on the playground at school—I blithely checked the next best alternative, "Other." "Wait," my dad said taking the clipboard from me before handing it to the government worker behind the glass partition. I was just tall enough to see him erase one checkmark and make another—right next to the box labeled "White."

I won't be so bold as to suggest that was the moment in which I decided to become a sociologist. But in hindsight, that moment did make two long-lasting impressions that have stuck with me to the present day. First, and most obvious to me back in the social security office, is the way those with greater power than ourselves can greatly limit the boundaries of who we think we are. Who was I to challenge my father's belief that we pertained to the white race, even though it seemed clear to me at the time that we were in fact "Others"? Second, I also got my first taste, back then in my sun soaked, Star Wars–addled youth, of the apparent disconnect between categories of race and people's actual appearance. Could my father, whose dark skin and indigenous features betrayed his own parents' migratory origins in central Mexico, really believe he looked white? It would not be until many years later that I would be able to put that moment in historical context—that I could see my father there in his mid-fifties, after having fought in World War II, after struggling to get promoted through a steel-workers union still tainted by racial discrimination, correcting his skinny inexperienced son, letting him know that to be "white" for his generation meant to be American.

In the pages that follow, "social construction" is one of the terms used to describe this sense that who we think we are is heavily dependent on social context, history, and what others have allowed us to be. "American Mestizaje" is the term I use specifically to refer to the social construction of Mexican ethnicity within the United States. The argument laid out in this book comes from a position of relative privilege—not in the economic sense, necessarily, but rather from the biographical sense of having experienced my own ethnicity through a kind of triangulation.

I am the fourth of five children in my family. Both my parents were of the World War II generation. As a child in the 1920s, my father attended segregated Catholic mass in the basement of St. Mary's Basilica in downtown Phoenix before the Mexican American community established its own church six blocks away. Both my parents would later attend segregated dances as young adults at the city's Riverside Ballroom in the late 1940s. After getting married in 1951 and settling in what was then the north side of town, they maintained close ties to their extended families, many of whom still lived in the more ethnically concentrated south side. Part of their civic life included membership in the League of United Latin American Citizens (LULAC). Theirs was an experience not unlike many working- and middle-class Mexican American families of the time: doing their best to provide for their children in a society that was not always so accepting of people who might possibly be identified as non-white.

My oldest brother and sister would come of age in a different period altogether, both of them entering college in the early 1970s. Though neither of them espoused particularly radical politics, outward expressions of ethnic pride such as style of dress, a portrait of Pancho Villa hanging from the wall, and the music of Malo and Santana blasting from the backroom let me know from an early age that being Mexican American could be pretty cool. Why would anyone ever want to identify as "white"?

My personal experience of ethnicity as an adult has been profoundly colored by a three-year stint in the U.S. Peace Corps in Latin America. Though I had always thought of myself as Mexican American, it wasn't until my time abroad in Costa Rica and Argentina that I realized just how American—as in, of the United States and its culture—I actually was. Thus, throughout my life, Mexican ethnicity has never meant one specific thing, but has instead been constantly changing from one period in time to the next, from one location to another. Even within the United States, people's perception of who I am is likely to depend on where I am—"Tom" or "Thomas" in my homeland of Arizona and New Mexico, while in Wisconsin, where I went to graduate school, and in Vermont, where I currently teach, people are much more likely to spontaneously address me as "Tomás." What gives? I don't have a definite answer, but little discrepancies like that, and the difference of opinion between my father and me way back when, have cumulatively led me down the path to *Mestizo in America* and the understanding that Mexican ethnicity is in large part determined by things much greater than our personal volition.

Acknowledgments

The research in this book could not have been realized without the generous contributions of time, insight, and then some from the many people I have gotten to know through my graduate education and since beginning this project in 2001. First and foremost, I extend my gratitude to the fifty men and women who took time out of their day to allow me into their home or place of work to talk for a few hours about what exactly Mexican ethnicity means to them. Speaking with strangers is not one of my great strengths, but I was always pleasantly surprised by how welcoming the people I interviewed were, and how eager they were to talk about a topic that, for some, is deeply personal and which, for most of us, is not a part of regular day-to-day conversation. Without them this research would not have been possible, and I owe them the biggest thanks.

I would also like to acknowledge an intellectual debt to the people I have met and spoken to about this project during my graduate and post-graduate experience. At the University of New Mexico, Beverly Burris, Gil Merkx, and Rich Wood all provided early encouragement and support for my career in sociology. Sylvia Rodriguez's graduate seminar on Southwestern Ethnography in the Department of Anthropology there was particularly rewarding and allowed me to cultivate some of the early versions of ideas that would eventually come to fruition in this book. To Felipe Gonzales I owe special thanks for his thoughtful mentorship and the candor with which he spoke of both sociology and academic life.

At the University of Wisconsin, Madison, Pam Oliver, Lincoln Quillian, and Hong Jiang were all generous with their time and helpful comments on earlier drafts of this work. Gary Sandefur and Mitch Duneier, in particular, provided expert guidance with regard to how to best parlay my graduate work into published form. Among my fellow graduate students, I would like to acknowledge the insight and companionship of Miguel Ceballos, William Lugo, Christine Overdevest, Devah Pager, Sharmila Rudrappa, and Mike Spittel. While carrying out this research at the University of

Wisconsin, I received funding through a Dissertation Improvement Grant from the National Science Foundation (SES-0101091).

At the University of Vermont (UVM), my current academic home, I would like to acknowledge the friendship and support of faculty in the Department of Sociology. Within the UVM community at large, my conversations with Yolanda Flores, Alice Fothergill, and Andrew Jones have been particularly insightful with regard to this project. And within the broader Burlington community, I would like to acknowledge my ongoing dialogue with Luis Tijerina.

The inspiration for *Mestizo in America* has deep roots. In this regard, I owe special gratitude to my family, scattered across the country as we are, for their love, support, and unflagging good sense of humor.

Mestizo in America

1 The Restricted Entry of a Forbidden Term

> When mixing has been problematic from the point of view of those who need to keep ethnic groups "pure," mestizaje as a distinct classification has simply been ignored.
>
> —J. Jorge Klor de Alva[1]

Where does *mestizaje* end? Why does this term connoting racial and cultural intermixture seem to refer only to a population residing somewhere to the south of the United States? Even the mass influx of immigrants from Latin America in recent decades has failed to see a simultaneous migration of the words *mestizo* or *mestiza* north to the United States. Some American sociologists have examined how mestizo identities must be rethought by Latin American immigrants in order to fit into our own particular categories of race and ethnicity. Many others have devoted their careers to understanding the socioeconomic status of former mestizos through their research on the "Latino" or "Hispanic" population. But few have considered how mestizaje as a practice of social and cultural intermixing continues over generations inside the United States. It is as though the intermingling of traditions and people so central to the Latino experience ends at the U.S.–Mexico border, or somewhere thereabouts.

Yet, one like myself, a third-generation Mexican American, need look no further than around the dinner table during the holidays to see the emptiness of this assumption. There, the "old" is mixed with the "new," the Mexicano with the Gringo. Everyone in my family—including married-in-Anglo and half-Anglo members—loves *tamales de elote* and my mother's flour tortillas. But a few of us also could not imagine Christmas dinner without canned cranberry sauce, the gelatinous kind that maintains its form after being plopped on a serving dish. And, unlike most of the extended family, every member of my immediate family detests *menudo* (Mexican tripe soup). Especially with regard to food, like the good American consumers we are, we consider our range of options and make a choice.

Our social world reflects a mixture as well, though one might question here the adequacy of a consumer options analogy. For example, though most of my siblings and I have Mexican American friends, we also tend to find ourselves in Anglo-majority work settings, and two of us have moved far away from our origins in Phoenix to places where Mexican Americans make up a relatively small portion of the local population. Our circles of friends and acquaintances reflect these geographic and place-specific facts. Thus, in addition to our affinity towards people on the basis of personality or cultural background, the social context within which we find ourselves determines to a large degree who we get to know and befriend, and even with whom we become romantically involved.

This is not to say that inter-group relations in the United States are simply a matter of numbers and relative group proportions. Social integration in this country has never been a matter of smoothly mixing or "melting" together people of different backgrounds into a unified whole. Other hard social facts, such as the history of discrimination against Mexican Americans in the Southwest and persistent social inequality between this group and the rest of the country with respect to education and income, set limits on the social and cultural "hybridization" of this rapidly growing subgroup of the population.

All claims to welcoming the world's tired, poor, and "huddled masses" aside, the acceptance of outside groups into American life has rarely come without a struggle. And for some groups this struggle has met with greater resistance than for others. When native-born Mexican Americans are harassed during a government "crackdown" on illegal immigration, such as happened in Chandler, Arizona, in the late 1990s, or when, as indicated by a few of the participants in the present study, college-educated Mexican Americans are mistaken for janitors or complimented by their coworkers for "not seeming Mexican," it becomes clear that not all groups are equally welcome into the fold of American society.

Part of the answer to the puzzle of the disappearing mestizo, then, is cultural dominance. From the perspective of non-Latinos in the United States, internal Latino diversity may be imperceptible—distinguishing Guatemaltecos from Nicaraguenses is like splitting so many hairs. The mainstream view dictates that the important cultural distinction between Anglos and Latinos is expressed most convincingly, if symbolically, through differences in language. The growing size of the Latino immigrant population in the Southwest and California, along with the conspicuous growth of Spanish-language media and businesses catering to the immigrant market, contribute to a sometimes distorted emphasis on the cultural division between Anglos and Latinos.

Even when government institutions, such as the U.S. Census Bureau, get beyond the iconic language split and allow Latinos to self-identify their ethnicity—Mexican, Puerto Rican, Cuban, or "Other"—key differences in immigrant generation, social class, and non-Latino ancestry go unmeasured or unreported in accounts of the present status of the "Hispanic population." The demographer's need for clearly delineated categories, and demands placed on the media to summarize complex national-level data for the average American consumer, both work to patrol mestizaje, ensuring that this increasingly relevant idea never ventures far from the southern borderland.

Confronted with the problem of unrecognized Latino diversity, a reasonable plan of attack from my own academic field, sociology, would involve amassing a variety of empirical data that would demonstrate the multiplicity of identities, lifestyles, and life chances found within the heterogeneous subpopulation of U.S. Latinos. For two reasons I am discouraged from taking that route. First, there are already a good number of books published for both academic audiences and popular consumption that provide exactly this panoramic view of Latino diversity, immigration, and adaptation to U.S. society.[2] Second, though in most cases an effort is made to distinguish among the many subgroups that constitute the larger group, one often comes away from these writings with the sense that adaptation, cross-group intermingling, and cultural mixing—dynamics I am placing under the umbrella category of mestizaje—are factors internal to Latino social life. My own experience as a Mexican American growing up in the Southwest and, in fact, national-level data related to changes over generations in intermarriage, occupations, and housing segregation tell me otherwise.[3] It appears that Latinos are becoming well woven into the fabric of American life, though in a way quite distinct from that of groups who have come before and from that of contemporary groups coming from other parts of the world.

My chosen strategy, then, is not to step back as one might to gaze upon the whole of an impressionist painting, but rather to step forward and examine the overlapping strokes of oil on a particular region of the canvas. Admittedly, as we near the point of interest for investigation our vision blurs, and it becomes more difficult to make out the larger forms we perceived when we stood farther away. But our approach is ultimately rewarding. Up close, we begin to understand how the work of integration gets done. This, after all, is where social interaction takes place, where people take what they are given and try to make something of it. Where individuals are included or excluded, identities are constructed or rejected, and mestizaje persists in the American present.

Specifically, this book focuses on the experience of social integration in a group given little attention in the sociological literature on race and ethnic relations—"third-plus" generation Mexican Americans. That is, Americans of Mexican origin whose families have been in the United States for at least three generations. Their near-absence in this research subfield is remarkable on a few counts. First, nearly seven million Mexican Americans currently share the defining third-plus-generation characteristic of having U.S.–born parents. Given the long history of migration from Mexico to the United States and the fact that most of what we now consider the American Southwest was once northern Mexico, this number should come as no surprise to anyone with some familiarity with American history. It certainly is no surprise to most Mexican Americans living in Arizona, California, Colorado, New Mexico, and Texas.

Second, this scholarly neglect has occurred over the last thirty years, during which time there has actually been quite a bit written about third-plus-generation adaptation, social integration, and ethnic identities. Unfortunately, the focus in this area of research has been almost exclusively on Americans of European ancestry. The general conclusion from these studies is that, despite an apparent surge in ethnic revivalism in the 1970s and 1980s and lingering evidence of "symbolic ethnicity," third- and fourth-generation European ethnics have, for the most part, been well integrated into the American mainstream and, through many measures including intermarriage, occupations, and political views, are hard to differentiate as distinct subgroups within the larger population.[4] Though sociologists working in this area often argue that the European American experience is clearly different from that of native-born minority groups, little effort is made to actually examine the experience of third-plus-generation Mexican Americans or that of other non-European groups with multiple-generation histories in the United States.[5]

Third, recent decades have also seen a dramatic increase in immigration from both Latin America and Asia. Concurrently, a growing sociological interest has emerged in trying to understand the unique qualities of post-1965 "new" immigration. The year 1965 is seen as key, since it was then that the last of a set of federal immigration laws was implemented, which set annual quotas that had contrasting effects on immigrant-origin groups. On the one hand, provisions that gave preferences for technically skilled workers and family reunification tended to open up immigration from Asia. These same laws, however, had the qualitatively different effect of setting strict limits on legal immigration from Latin America at a time when demand for low-wage, low-skill labor, especially in the U.S. service sector, was on the rise. Immigration from much of Latin America, but especially from Mexico, would become strongly tied in the popular imagination to the question of legal citizenship.

These changes in the immigration laws, combined with the racial distinctiveness of Latin American and Asian immigrant groups and changes in the U.S. economy related to the disappearance of relatively stable working-class jobs, have led to an academic debate in sociology regarding the fate of these "new" groups, who face social and economic circumstances very different from that of the "old" European groups that arrived in the earlier part of the twentieth century.[6] Missing from this discussion, however, is the fate of Latinos and Asian Americans whose grandparents and great-grandparents also arrived in the earlier part of the twentieth century or prior. It seems obvious that a good understanding of the differences between pre- and post-1965 immigration should address the experience of these groups that contain both "old" and "new" members.

My underlying goal of understanding how mestizaje persists in the present-day among third-plus-generation Mexican Americans also allows me to address some of the central issues occupying social scientists concerned with the way immigrant groups and their descendants are incorporated into American life. There are, of course, limits to the way the findings of this study of a particular portion of the Mexican-origin population can be generalized to the experience of other contemporary ethnic groups. It is, however, a good starting point and a necessary check on the generalizations of others working in this area of race and ethnic relations who may not be altogether familiar with the experience of the people I have chosen to write about.

My central argument is that, though the process of social integration for third-plus-generation Mexican Americans shares many elements with that of third-plus-generation European Americans, social forces related to ethnic concentration, social inequality, and identity politics have combined to make ethnicity for Mexican Americans more fixed across generations than it has been for other groups with multiple-generation histories in the United States. There are four major components to this argument, which I will briefly outline below.

First, long-term, ongoing immigration from Mexico creates a particular context for third-plus-generation Mexican Americans that is unique among the descendants of immigrants within the United States. Whereas high-volume immigration from Europe came to an end in the 1920s, immigration from Mexico has increased since that period, reaching its zenith during the 1990s when, it is now estimated, over three million Mexican immigrants arrived in the country.[7] The proximity of the United States to Mexico, the economic disparity between the two countries, and the dependence of the United States economy on low-wage labor have contributed to making ongoing Mexican immigration and the ethnic concentration it engenders a distinguishing aspect of Mexican American life throughout the twentieth century.

Using national data on Mexican/Anglo intermarriage as a measure, I argue that one effect of Mexican ethnic concentration, rooted in ongoing immigration, is higher levels of social distance between the Mexican-origin population and Anglos in the Southwest and California than are found in other parts of the country where concentrations are relatively low. This finding is consistent with social theories related to group size and social structure, which argue that smaller groups are more readily integrated into the dominant population than larger groups.[8] At the interpersonal level, comments from the people I interviewed show that inter-group social distance is also apparent in the way faulty assumptions regarding national origin, cultural knowledge, and ethnic identity are made about third-plus-generation Mexican Americans. Although these assumptions were often shrugged off as ignorance on the part of the person making them, at times the Mexican Americans I spoke with sensed a degree of devaluation of Mexican ethnicity in these expressions, especially when assurances were provided that it was "okay" to be Mexican. These kinds of interactions suggest that ongoing immigration tends to create a heightened, if distorted, awareness of ethnicity among the population in general, such that prejudice and stereotypes against groups experiencing ongoing immigration are maintained over time.

The flip side of ethnic concentration is that it also tends to reinforce Mexican American identity by providing greater opportunity to interact with fellow ethnics. In geographically vast metropolitan areas such as Phoenix and San Jose, California, where nearly a third of the population is of Mexican origin, this means that, though you may live and work in predominantly Anglo environments, ethnic networks of family, friends, and professionals across the urban and suburban landscape operate to reinforce ethnic identity, even outside the highly concentrated urban ethnic enclave. Thus, the mere size of the Mexican-origin population in the Southwest and California provides a steady source of ethnic fixity not broadly available to descendants of European immigrants.

A second source closely related to the fact of Mexican ethnic concentration and, more broadly, the growth of the Latino population throughout the United States, comes from ethnic culture acquired outside the ethnic community. That is, whereas American ethnic groups in the past have had to depend internally on ethnic institutions and geographically specific enclaves in urban areas for the perpetuation of ethnic culture, many of the third-plus-generation Mexican Americans I spoke with have ready access to Latino and Mexican culture in its mediated form found on television, on radio, and through other "cultural institutions." These forms of "disembedded" culture, made possible through the modern commercial tools of electronic media, as well as the scholarly study of culture and language, facilitate the "imagining" of Mexican ethnicity that can occur without having to actually live within an ethnically concentrated community.

A third source of fixity emerged from the racial and ethnic identity movements of the 1960s and 1970s. Social researchers of race and ethnicity have argued that Black Power, the Chicano Movement, and other social movements from that era worked to invert ethnic and racial status from a form of social stigma to a source of group pride.[9] Chicano activists in particular rejected the assimilationist expectations espoused by mainstream society and, in many cases, by their own World War II–generation parents. In doing so they worked to radicalize the Civil Rights Movement's demand of desegregation and equality before the law for historically aggrieved groups to one of recognition, recompense, and even separatism on the basis of racial and ethnic identities. Ongoing racism and cultural resistance on the part of minorities themselves, it was felt, made it unlikely they would blend any time soon with the white majority.

A key policy outcome of these identity-based movements was changes in federal law designed to improve the representation of minorities at the workplace and in higher education. Though Affirmative Action policies have never garnered broad political support among the U.S. population as a whole and have met with much political opposition in recent years, they have worked to dramatically change the structure of integration of minorities into higher education and middle-class occupations.[10]

Whereas before outside groups faced overwhelming pressure to conform to Anglo American norms and leave behind or, at the very least, keep private their ethnic affiliations, minority status is now a public aspect of professional life and social identity, a fact made clear by the ethnic identity professional organizations many of the people interviewed for this book participated in. Based on their awareness of socioeconomic disparity between Mexican Americans and Anglos, the low representation of Mexican Americans at the workplace, and persistent stereotypes and prejudice held against this group by the broader population, the majority of the respondents in this study were in favor of Affirmative Action policies that take into consideration racial and ethnic identity, despite the occasional doubt-inducing encounter with accusations of "reverse discrimination."

Lastly, considerable evidence shows that since the middle part of the twentieth century, the United States has experienced greater inequality. Sociologists comparing the post-1965 pattern of immigration and social integration to that of the earlier part of the century often point to the segmented nature of the economy, which makes it increasingly difficult for the descendants of immigrants arriving with few job skills and little education to attain the kind of economic advancement attained by the descendants of European immigrants. "Segmented assimilation" theory posits that the deindustrialization of the U.S. economy has meant the disappearance of stable, well-paying, often unionized working-class jobs. In the past, these positions provided the crucial cross-generational link between the hardship endured by recently arrived immigrants and the middle-class status of their third-plus-generation descendants.

Referring again to the intermarriage data, average differences in educational attainment between Anglos and Mexican Americans is another key factor in predicting the likelihood of this important measure of social distance between two groups within a metropolitan area. This finding, like that of the effects of ethnic concentration, is consistent with a sociological understanding of inter-group relations, as well. Specifically, higher levels of inequality between two groups will tend to lower the chances that between-group interaction will occur, thus lowering the likelihood of integration.[11] This suggests that if we continue to live in the present stratified society, in which there is decreasing opportunity for economic advancement, and if the multiple-generation Mexican-origin population continues to disproportionately occupy its lower strata, we may expect that levels of social distance between Mexican Americans and the dominant society will be higher than those between the dominant society and other ethnic groups who were integrated during historical periods with comparatively lower levels of social inequality.

Data and Methods

This study uses two major sources of data. The first is an annual national survey, known as the Current Population Survey, taken by the U.S. Census Bureau and the Department of Labor Statistics. This will be discussed in greater detail in chapter 4, where I provide a broad, demographic perspective on Mexican American integration by considering national-level trends related to social class, regional differences in ethnic group concentration, and Mexican-origin/Anglo intermarriage.

The scale of most of the data prepared for this book, however, is ethnographic as you might expect coming from a researcher investigating the more ambiguous aspects of official categories of race and ethnicity. Thus, in the spring and summer of 2001 I spoke with a total of fifty third-plus-generation Mexican Americans about their experience of social integration in the Phoenix, Arizona, and San Jose, California, metro areas. These interview data, a more fine-grained description of which follows, provide the basis for chapters 2, 3, and 5.

Given the study's focus on the social integration of third-plus-generation Mexican Americans, I deliberately sought out potential interviewees who had experience living and working in what I call "integrating environments"—places where third-plus-generation Mexican Americans can expect to encounter the most contact, intimate and otherwise, with the dominant society. The following description of selection criteria should help clarify this point. First, the participants were people of Mexican ancestry with parents born in the United States. That is, all participants had at least one Mexican-origin parent born in the United States. In six cases, participants had one parent born in Mexico, making them part second generation. In those cases I "rounded up" and included them on the basis of their third-plus-generation parentage. Mexican ancestry is defined here as having at least one Mexican American parent. Given the growing percentage of Mexican Americans of mixed ancestry, and especially among the younger cohorts, I made sure that approximately a quarter of the sample had one non-Mexican-origin parent. This is consistent with the national average of intermarriage for native-born Mexican Americans, which is 25 percent.[12]

Second, those interviewed were between the ages of twenty-five and forty-five. The lower limit was used to include those who have likely finished their formal schooling and have at least a few years of experience in the adult workforce. The upper limit was set to focus on those who reached adulthood after the Immigration Act of 1965, which marked the beginning of the present period of high Latin American immigration into the United States. This group also grew up after the height of the ethnic identity movements of the late-1960s and early-1970s. By the time these individuals reached adulthood, the major accomplishments of the Chicano and Civil Rights Movements were historical facts whose symbolic impact on their identity depended more on learned knowledge than direct experience. Presumably, this is an aspect of integration into American cultural life that they will share with future third-plus-generation Mexican Americans.

The third and, superficially, most unusual aspect of this sample is that almost all of the participants lived in the suburbs. This, however, is not as surprising as it may sound. Presently, 47.8 percent of the Mexican-origin population in the United States lives in the suburbs, a level similar to that of other Latino and Asian groups.[13] The process of spatial integration for Mexican Americans is similar to that of other groups, with the probability of having a suburban residence and residential contact with non–Mexican Americans increasing substantially with rising education, income, occupational status, and improving English language ability among the foreign born.[14] The emphasis in this study on suburban residence is consistent with other research that has examined the optional nature of ethnicity among other third-plus-generation ethnic groups.[15]

Fourth, consistent with the study's focus on integrating environments, all the project participants have had at least some college education, a status attained by approximately 37 percent of the third-plus-generation Mexican American population.[16] The sample thus includes a range of educational experiences, from high school graduates to those with graduate degrees. In most cases, these individuals have had contact with one of the most integrating institutions in American life, as reflected in the high levels of intermarriage among Latinos with college degrees.[17]

This last point, it should be acknowledged, is a kind of two-sided coin. *De un lado*, the selection of interviewees affords us a unique perspective from a subgroup of Mexican Americans whose lives regularly transgress boundaries of culture and identity at work, school, and, especially in the case of mixed ethnic families, in the home. *Del otro lado*, in gaining this perspective we must also acknowledge the pervasive barriers of social class, revealed here most clearly in terms of educational attainment. Discouraging high school dropout rates and relatively low levels of college graduation across generations have come to define the Mexican American population as overwhelmingly working class, making the people interviewed for this study on the whole an exception to the rule. Keeping in mind this bias of selection, it is perhaps all the more remarkable that most of the people I interviewed for this study felt a strong identification with their working-class roots, maintaining what one author has called the "Chicano ethos," despite having attained a degree of upward class mobility. This particular aspect of American Mestizaje is addressed directly in chapter 3.

One final matter concerning the study participants should be considered while assimilating the contents of this book. To maintain confidentiality and to, I hope, attain a level of frankness not otherwise attainable, the names of all interviewees cited in the following chapters have been changed. Further information regarding selected interview characteristics, the interview schedule, and the sample selection of interviewees may be found in Appendixes I, II, and III.

The American Context of Mestizaje: A Brief Overview

Before examining the persistence of mestizaje in the present-day United States, it might be helpful to consider some of the key social forces behind the transnational movement of mestizos from Mexico to the United States over the past hundred years or so. To begin with, it must be acknowledged that Mexican American history and the United States' settlement of the West are profoundly intertwined. Each heavily constitutes the other. Much as late-nineteenth-century immigrants from eastern and southern Europe provided the low-wage labor necessary for industrial growth in the Northeast and upper Midwest, early twentieth-century Mexican immigrants provided the essential labor for the expansion of railroads, mining, and industrial agriculture in the American Southwest. Of the fifty third-plus-generation Mexican Americans I spoke with, all but six had ancestors that arrived in the United States between 1900 and 1930, a time of extraordinary transformation within the Mexican republic.

Revolution in Mexico and the "Great Migration" North

A steady flow of Mexican migrants came to the United States during the second half of the nineteenth century, and many thousands of Mexican citizens already resided in what would become the American Southwest before the region was ceded to the United States by Mexico in 1848. But what is sometimes referred to by Chicano scholars as the Mexican Great Migration did not begin in earnest until the beginning of the Mexican Revolution. This social, cultural, and economic upheaval—a true revolution in every sense of the word—was triggered in 1910 by the contested reelection of longtime dictator Porfirio Diaz. Revolutionary leaders, including Francisco Madero, Pancho Villa, and Emiliano Zapata, sought initially the redistribution of land and political power that had become through the course of the Diaz regime concentrated in the hands of foreign investors and Mexican elites. Successful as the Revolution was in toppling the thirty-six-year-long "Porfiriato," it left in its wake a wave of devastation.[18]

In all, over 1.5 million lives were lost in Mexico between 1910 and 1920 as the Revolution devolved in many parts of the country into chaos.[19] As the struggle became more ruthless, large numbers of peasants—who may have only considered migration in the past—made the decision that life in El Norte might be a better alternative than the extreme economic insecurity and social instability they faced in Mexico. As Phil, a thirty-five-year-old marketing manager living in Phoenix recalls: "My grandfather first came to Arizona to earn money to buy a ranch down in Jalisco. And he did that, went back, married my grandmother, bought a ranch, and was then chased off the ranch, he claims, by Villistas [supporters of northern revolutionary leader Pancho Villa]. Whether they were actually Villistas or not, I don't know. He seemed to claim that any band of renegades were Villistas. After that, he became quite fearful and never went back to Mexico."

Post-Revolutionary Life and Work in the American Southwest

Though life in the United States may have seemed a great improvement over the bedlam of revolutionary Mexico, the move north across the border could not have been an easy one. In much of the Southwest, racist beliefs fostered during the U.S.–Mexican War (1846–1848) and the period that followed held that Mexicans were unintelligent, lazy, and generally inferior to whites. In addition to legitimizing acts of violence against Mexicans in the southwestern borderlands, such beliefs justified and helped perpetuate a dual-wage system of labor that took its most severe form in mining and agriculture.[20] In the case of agriculture, this meant an occupationally stratified system through which Mexican labor, instead of getting paid less for the same work, simply occupied the lowest paying positions. In both mining and agriculture an ethnically split labor market worked in the favor of corporate owners as it tended to lower the likelihood of unionization. There is, in fact, clear evidence that efforts were made on the part of Arizona cotton farmers in the early 1900s to recruit and maintain an oversupply of Mexican immigrants, thus assuring wages could be kept as low as possible.[21]

Of course, European immigrants in other parts of the country were also taken advantage of on the basis of their subordinate status and lack of familiarity with U.S. society. However, a central distinction should be made between the two experiences. Namely, the vast majority of Europeans who migrated to the United States in the first part of the twentieth century settled in the nation's largest cities. Though these immigrants often lived in the margins of American society, impoverished and politically powerless, their children, nevertheless, grew up in an urban environment. There, in addition to the support they received from their own ethnic community in the form of mutual aid societies, job networks, and political organization, they were exposed to many of the benefits associated with city life. These included public education, access to libraries and museums, participation in civic and cultural activities, and an array of employment opportunities unavailable to their immigrant parents.

In contrast, most Mexicans working in mining, railroad construction, and agriculture led comparably isolated lives far away from urban centers. Even after arriving in the United States, migration for many Mexican workers became a way of life. In farm-worker families, children were much more likely to be laboring in the fields with their parents than receiving classroom instruction. To this day, the children of farm workers suffer from the migratory nature of the work, which requires them to move from one part of the country to another throughout the year in a pattern poorly matched to the schedule of the academic calendar. The Mexican American population in the first half of the twentieth century, as historian Manuel Gonzales has stressed, was highly transient.[22]

Vera, a high school math instructor I spoke with in San Jose told me the following about her grandparents' itinerant lifestyle: "On my dad's side, his father came over when he was three, and his mother grew up in Texas. They only had about a third grade education. They were migrant workers. They followed the fields from California to Michigan and Texas." Even those who resided part of the year in major urban areas, such as Los Angeles, would migrate to other parts of the country to follow the seasonal pattern of agricultural crops. The family farm model epitomized by northern European-origin homesteaders in the Midwest was abandoned in the American Southwest. There, the possession of massive tracts of land by

industrial farmers required an enormous pool of seasonal low-wage workers to make the enterprise profitable. Mexican immigrants fleeing the social unrest of the Mexican Revolution provided the bulk of that labor pool
during the first decades of the twentieth century.

Migration as a lifestyle, however, was not limited to those working in
industrial agriculture, nor to internal seasonal migration within the United
States. Miners also found themselves moving to locations where their
skills, often learned in Mexico, were needed. Jerry, a thirty-eight-year-old
Phoenix resident who grew up in a small mining community in Arizona, recalls what he learned of his grandparents' migration to the United States:

> Jerry: My dad's family came up to do mining, but the extended family
> split up to all the different mines in Arizona. My father's grandfather
> was a miner as well, and they would come up ahead of the family to
> work in the mines in Arizona and then go back.
>
> TM: Do you know why they left Mexico?
>
> Jerry: I think it was to work. My family has a history of copper miners,
> so they were people who did mining in Mexico and had the skill set,
> and they were recruited with a lot of other people to come and work
> in the mines.

Of the 111 occupations the people I spoke with knew their grandparents
held, nearly half were in farm labor (32 percent) and mining (17 percent).
In addition to mining and migrant farm labor, Mexican American workers
in the 1920s were concentrated in railroad construction and in blue-collar
urban jobs, such as building construction, metal and wood manufacturing,
and food processing.[23] Looking at urban occupations, social historian Mario Barrera argues that even though Mexican Americans held service and
skilled positions in the cities of the Southwest, there is little evidence that
they were integrated with Anglo workers. Skilled workers from Mexico,
for example, usually did not or were not allowed to join unions, and they often found themselves in the position of having to move down to non-skilled
positions or restrict the use of their skills to Mexican-origin clientele.[24]

The onset of the Great Depression only intensified the exclusion of
Mexican Americans from better paying work and sharpened the bitter-
ness held towards them by Anglos, who now feared more than ever a
fierce competition for jobs. This particular variant of xenophobia culminated tragically in the government-sponsored repatriation of over half a
million Mexican immigrants back to Mexico during the 1930s. The pos-

sibility of a better life for the children of the Great Migration generation would now depend in large part on post-war economic growth in the cities of the Southwest and California. Two of these metropolitan areas—the sites where I conducted interviews for this study—are considered in the following sections.

Farming, Flooding, and Segregation in "The Valley of the Sun"

The establishment of Phoenix in the Salt River Valley of southern Arizona came rather late in the history of U.S. settlement of the West. The need for a stable supply of provisions for Fort McDowell and various mining camps in central Arizona created a demand for regional agriculture. This was soon met by the Anglo settlers of Phoenix who began developing the region in the mid-1860s. From the beginning, much of the agricultural and manual labor required in the settlement was provided by Mexicans, most of whom had migrated up from the northern Mexican state of Sonora.[25]

When the Great Flood of 1891 made it clear that some parts of the desert valley were better situated than others, a noted pattern of racial and class segregation emerged, which persists today. The minority working-class population consisting mainly of Mexican-origin people, but which also included blacks and a small Chinese community, was concentrated south of the railroad tracks near the river basin. Meanwhile, the wealthier Anglo population was concentrated in self-segregated neighborhoods on the northern side of town.[26] Through the post–World War II period, Anglos and Mexican Americans in Phoenix lived separate lives. As Phoenix historian Bradford Luckingham notes:

> Throughout Anglo Phoenix signs warned, "No Mexicans Allowed." Or when Mexicans were allowed, they were restricted to certain days: Mexican day at local swimming pools; Mexican night at the Riverside Ballroom; the *Arizona Republic*'s picnic for "Mexican kiddies" only. As one observer later recalled, "Discrimination went from the church, parks, schools, hotels, theaters—the whole spectrum of rights was permeated by discrimination."[27]

In the Phoenix public school system, the segregation of white and Mexican American children was justified on the basis of "language deficiencies." This was standard practice until the Arizona State Supreme Court ruled it to be a violation of the Fourteenth Amendment in 1952.[28]

From Spanish Colonies to Del Monte Canneries
in "The Valley of Heart's Delight"

Established nearly a century prior to Phoenix in 1777, San Jose also served initially as a source of agricultural provisions for nearby outposts; in this case, the Spanish colonial presidios of Monterey and San Francisco.[29] Due to the relatively low numbers of Spanish settlers and a colonial culture that promoted the religious conversion of non-Christians, early settlement of San Jose was marked by a high degree of intermarriage between Europeans and the local population of Ohlone Indians.[30] By the early nineteenth century, mestizaje in Alta California had considerably blurred the lines of racial difference in the population. From the colonizers' point of view, the more important distinction among those living within the Spanish territory was religious and cultural—between the enlightened "gente de razon," and the savage "indios barbaros." That this was a cultural division largely dependent on one's degree of assimilation and religious faith did not lessen the violence that occasionally erupted between these two groups over the control of land and natural resources.[31]

Racial lines continued to blur into the period of Mexican independence from Spain. By 1845, one-sixth of the 900 residents of San Jose were Anglo Americans, and between 1821 and 1846, two-thirds of Anglo men living there married Mexican women.[32] The signing of the Treaty of Guadalupe Hidalgo in 1848 marked the beginning of United States rule and Anglo domination of the region. Drawn to northern California, initially by the prospect of agricultural development and later by the region's mineral wealth, Anglo American settlers rapidly displaced native "Californios" from their position of relative political and economic power in the second half of the nineteenth century. It was during this period that the ideology of white supremacy took hold among the white working class. Violence against American Indians, Chinese Americans, and Mexican Americans grew, and their exclusion from all but the lowest paying, most grueling jobs in mining and agriculture set a precedent that would color race relations up and through the next century.[33]

The first decades of the twentieth century saw continuing growth in demand for agricultural labor, as well as the emergence of the lucrative canning industry in San Jose. This last development resulted in a rush of Mexican immigration to the South Bay area during World War II.[34] By the 1950s, San Jose was home to dozens of fruit and vegetable canneries, most notably Del Monte, which became central nodes of employment for working-class Mexican Americans. Not unlike the ethnic communities of Phoenix, the concentration of San Jose's Mexican American population was near a flood zone in a part of the city known as East San Jose. And as was the case in much of the Southwest at mid-century, housing segregation in San Jose was maintained by a mixture of economic factors tied to income and wealth and overt discrimination manifest in housing covenants that forbade non-whites from living in restricted neighborhoods.

Mexican American Civic Participation in the Post-War Era

By the mid-1950s, de facto segregation against Mexican Americans in theaters, restaurants, and other public spaces was on the decline in cities throughout the Southwest. Such changes, in part, reflected the growth and emerging political influence of the Mexican American middle class. Upon returning from a war fought in defense of liberty against fascist states in Europe and Asia, many Mexican American G.I.s expected equal treatment and at least a modicum of respect from their home country. To this end, Mexican veterans and their families throughout the Southwest joined ethnic-based organizations such as the G.I. Forum, the League of United Latin American Citizens (LULAC), and the Alianza Hispano Americana. Such groups were largely assimilationist in their missions in that their primary goal was the attainment of equal rights for Mexican American citizens and their integration into mainstream American society through education and economic opportunity.[35] In this way, their goals were largely consistent with those of the broader Civil Rights Movement rising to national prominence at the time.

Membership in ethnic identity organizations, however, was but one way socially mobile Mexican Americans expressed their civic-mindedness during this period. In his set of San Francisco Bay area case studies, *City Against Suburb: The Cultural Wars in an American Metropolis,* Rodriguez (1999) accounts the efforts Mexican American professionals made in the late 1960s to revive the annual Fiesta de las Rosas in San Jose.[36] Fiesta supporters, which included many Mexican Americans of the World War II generation, sought to promote a stronger sense of civic pride and identity by celebrating the contributions of Anglos, Mexicans, and Spaniards to the city's history. Unfortunately for the Fiesta planners, the Fiesta parade would come literally face-to-face with a new generation of Mexican American youth who rejected precisely such a harmonious account of regional history.

The Chicano Challenge

In the 1960s and 1970s, the children of the G.I. generation became prominent on the political scene. For many Mexican American youth living in
the U.S. Southwest, this meant a rejection of their parents' assimilationist
ideals and an embracing of a working-class Chicano identity. In the case
of the Fiestas de las Rosas parade of 1969, about 100 Chicano youth wear-
ing black berets crashed the procession in protest. They carried placards
and shouted their disapproval of the parade's portrayal of a rancher on
horseback driving a Mexican "peon" on foot. At some point, the protesters
walked into a blockade of police officers who, wielding their night sticks,
made thirty arrests. A dozen protesters and three officers were injured.[37]

In the Phoenix area, the Mexican American Student Organization
(MASO) promoted student activism on the Tempe campus of Arizona
State University while Chicanos por la Causa (CPLC) sought to improve
the living conditions of Mexican Americans living in Phoenix barrios.[38]
Citing a lack of attention to the needs of minority students, the CPLC organized a parent-student boycott of Phoenix Union High School in the
fall of 1970. Through the 1950s and 1960s, the downtown Phoenix Union
campus had deteriorated as the Anglo portion of the student body dwin-
dled to less than 20 percent.[39] Minority students, according to the boycott
leaders, were being tracked to learn manual labor rather than intellectual
skills, thus perpetuating ethnic discrimination. In response, school officials promised to hire more minority faculty and be more receptive to the
needs of minority students.[40]

Inspired by both Civil Rights Era politics and the organizing successes
of the Cesar Chavez–led United Farm Workers Union, Chicano Movement
organizations flourished in the early 1970s. Groups originating from the
student movement at the time, such as MASO and MAPA (the Mexican
American Political Association), and community-level organizations, such
as CPLC and MACSA (the Mexican American Community Service Agency), would serve as the early training ground for many Mexican American
community and political leaders in San Jose and Phoenix from that moment on.

Suburban Sprawl and the Return of Xenophobia

Dramatic growth in the cities of the Sunbelt has not affected all groups
equally. In the case of the Golden Gate neighborhood in south Phoenix,

the expansion of Sky Harbor International Airport resulted in the demolition of one of the city's oldest Mexican American communities in the early 1980s.[41] In the barrios that remained, decaying schools, slum housing, and low employment opportunities contributed to the growth in popularity of street gangs in the 1980s and early 1990s. In the area in and around San Jose, now popularly referred to as the Silicon Valley, the booming tech economy of the 1990s and its aftermath have sent the real estate market spiraling upward, pricing many Mexican-origin families out of the housing market. The result has been higher concentrations of Mexican Americans and other more recent immigrant groups from Central America and parts of Southeast Asia in the relatively less expensive housing stock of East San Jose.

Though both the Phoenix and San Jose metro areas have seen growth in the size of the Mexican American middle class over the past thirty years, the predominantly first- and second-generation working class has grown even faster. Mass immigration to the Sunbelt since 1965 has itself been spurred in good measure by the phenomenal economic growth of its cities. This is especially obvious in sectors of the economy such as housing construction and low-wage services for the middle-class, including childcare, domestic labor, landscaping, food preparation, and hospitality.

Curiously, many of the same people who have benefited directly from low-cost immigrant labor have rallied, in a now predictable pattern, against liberal immigration policy. In 1994, near the end of an economic recession begun in the first Bush administration, California voters, including a good number of non-immigrant Latinos, enthusiastically supported Proposition 187, an initiative designed to cut immigrant families off from public benefits in medical care, welfare, and education. A very similar measure, Proposition 200, was passed by Arizona voters during the 2004 presidential election. After four years of rocky economic growth that benefited primarily the wealthy while working-class wages deteriorated, the Arizona electorate apparently felt more comfortable scapegoating undocumented immigrants than blaming either the businesses that hire them or top officials in government for the current level of economic insecurity.[42]

Much has been made of the level of the Latino support for recent anti-immigration initiatives (23 percent of Latino voters for Prop. 187, and 47 percent for Prop. 200).[43] Arguably, however, the more remarkable outcome in both California and Arizona has been the galvanizing effect anti-immigration politics has had among Mexican Americans who, though they may be American citizens themselves, identify and sympathize with

the struggles of first-generation families. In the case of California, it is estimated that the passage of 187 in 1994 led to an unprecedented registration
of Latino voters as Democrats for the 1996 election.[44] And a December
2004 edition of the Phoenix-based *Arizona Republic* reports,

> The passage of Proposition 200 has set off a wave of activism among
> Arizona's young Latinos, a level not seen since the Chicano Movement
> of the 1960s. Back then, young Latinos engaged for the first time in
> boycotts, marches, and fasts in support of social justice. . . . The new
> groundswell of activism involves their children, who feel threatened
> by Proposition 200 and fear what it could mean for them, their parents,
> and the future of Latinos in Arizona.[45]

The article goes on to describe some of the cross-generational activism
emerging among former Chicano Movement leaders now working in government and business and present-day student activists. Speaking to the
solidarity he sees between himself and recent Mexican immigrants, one
of the students, a construction major at Arizona State University, asserts,
"If you offend one of them, you offend me. Now that [Proposition 200]
passed, hopefully we can motivate even more people."[46]

As this brief summary suggests, mestizaje is an identity in process, a
product of the historical struggle for material resources, social justice, and
political representation. It straddles the border between the United States
and Mexico, and it is marked by its own internal legacy of alliances and
divisions. At times we see brought into relief the chasm of generations, acculturation, and social class that can separate one group of Mexican Americans from another. At other times, political necessity and a shared sense
of social exclusion from mainstream society draw our focus to a common
mestizo history and the interconnected continuity of our lives.

Layout of the Book

The layout of the book is directly tied to classical assumptions in sociology about the social integration and adaptation of U.S. ethnic and racial subgroups. Namely, acculturation makes possible the integration of
ethnic groups into mainstream institutions (structural assimilation). This
new proximity to people outside a given ethnic group, in turn, facilitates
inter-group relationships, including intermarriage, which itself eventually
results in the loss of ethnic identity (identity assimilation). In each of the
following chapters, though the classical statement goes far in helping us

understand the contemporary experience of third-plus-generation Mexican Americans, I find it is insufficient, and I work to fill in the gaps with more recent insights from sociological research.

Beginning with cultural assimilation, interview responses in chapter 2 with regard to language loss and conformity to societal expectations of gender roles, for example, suggest that classical expectations of acculturation hold true for socially integrated third-plus-generation Mexican Americans. Referring to Benedict Anderson's 1983 writing on "imagined communities," however, I argue that "mediated culture," in the form of Spanish-language television and learning opportunities provided by cultural institutions in the ethnically concentrated Southwest and California, have helped to sustain the "imagining" of Mexican American ethnicity even after certain cultural practices strongly associated with this identity have long been abandoned. By using an "imaginary" approach in this analysis, I deliberately attempt to downplay thinking about culture as a set of "traits" or fixed characteristics that define a cultural subgroup. Instead, I focus on how the people I spoke with utilize available cultural resources—specifically, religion, spoken Spanish, cross-national encounters, and Spanish-language television—to reinforce and recreate Mexican ethnicity in their day-to-day lives.

In chapter 3, the predicted confluence of acculturation with structural assimilation is supported by the responses of Mexican American professionals who acknowledge the need to conform to dominant culture expectations, both inside and outside the workplace, in order to fit in and hopefully advance their careers. I argue, however, that because of changes in the structure of structural assimilation since 1965, most notably with relation to identity politics, Affirmative Action policy, and voluntary organizations, integration into the society's dominant institutions no longer requires checking your ethnicity at the door. Ethnic identity professional organizations in particular provide a key source of ethnic networking for many of the Mexican American professionals I spoke with who typically find themselves in work settings with low levels of minority representation.

Principally because of the ready availability of national-level data in this area, I turn to the quantitative analysis of Mexican/Anglo intermarriage in chapter 4. Using immigrant generation as a measure of acculturation and educational attainment as a measure of structural assimilation, I am able to confirm the predicted positive correlation these two individual-level factors have with the probability of out-marriage from an ethnic group. However, in the statistical models, I also include metro-area-level measures of ethnic concentration and inter-group status inequality, which contribute additional precision to the analysis. Regional variation in these structural factors rooted in the historical process of ongoing immigration from Mexico, I argue, point to the inadequacy of the broad application of classical assimilation theory to the Mexican-origin population residing throughout the United States.

In chapter 5, I return to the interview data to examine the meaning of ethnic identity among third-plus-generation Mexican Americans. The old expectations of identity assimilation have been criticized for many years by researchers who point to the long-term symbolic strength of ethnicity, even for those of multiple ethnic origins whose families arrived in the United States generations ago. For some of the respondents, especially those of mixed ethnic background, there is evidence that ethnicity is, to a large degree, symbolic or "optional" as they are able to easily adjust their ethnic identity with respect to the social context. However, based on the respondents' comments and referring to recent work on social constructionism, I argue that Mexican American identity is not merely another among various ethnic options available in U.S. culture. Instead, certain stereotypes and expectations are still associated with this identity, which make it less than voluntary, and these are evident in social interactions that take place between Mexican Americans and Anglos.

Chapter 6 concludes the study with a historical perspective on the changing significance of mestizaje from seventeenth century New Spain to the present-day United States. I argue here that mestizaje as a concept helps draw our attention to the ambiguity apparent within official categories of race and ethnicity, while reminding us how social inequality, ethnic concentration, and political opportunity have operated historically to imbue racial and ethnic ambiguity with historically specific meaning. Lessons from the past and our knowledge of the present, I argue, afford us a cautious glimpse of what American Mestizaje might mean to us over the coming decades.

2 Imagining Mexican American Culture

Dan: I want to play in a mariachi band. I can't speak the language very well, but maybe I could play a little music. I want to put on the hat and the pants and I want to play the horn and sing the songs. I'm very serious about this. I'm taking a course taught by an instructor at the Mexican Heritage Corporation in San Jose, and I'm working hard at it. So, I'm one of those people who are right on the line. I'm a professional, and I still have all these roots I'm connected to, and I'm not letting go. I'm a statistical oddity.
—From interview with Dan, Silicon Valley engineer

Alex: But, on my dad's side, it's not defined enough, like I think we're Eastern European, maybe Lithuanian. I don't know how to identify with that at all. I mean, what do I do? Celebrate Lithuanian Day? I don't know if there's an instrument that I need to be playing. I don't know how to bind myself to that culture.
—From interview with Alex, half-Mexican small-business owner in the Phoenix area

Dan's and Alex's comments quoted above point to the meaningful context within which ethnicity is experienced as a part of everyday life. In San Jose, California, where cultural institutions such as the Mexican Heritage Corporation exist, Dan, who speaks little Spanish and lives and works in Anglo-majority environments, can pursue his dream of playing backup for a mariachi band and feel "connected" to his cultural roots. Alex, on the other hand, does not even know where to begin to "bind" himself to his Lithuanian heritage. If there is an authentic Lithuanian musical instrument for him to play, he does not know what it is, and chances are there would not be many Lithuanian bands to play with near where he lives in Scottsdale, anyway. It is clear that his social context, in comparison to Dan's, leaves his imagination of Lithuanian culture at a serious disadvantage. And, according to recent developments in social theory, "imagination" is indeed the operative term.

Imagined Communities of Nations and Ethnicity

In trying to find an explanation for the rise of nationalism in the eighteenth century that did not depend on a mythical understanding of group origins, social theorist Benedict Anderson arrived at the notion of the "imagined community."[1] He argued that national communities were imagined because, though members of a country or nation do not actually know all other members personally, they still manage to believe they share among themselves a common heritage and destiny. In contrast to what might take place in a small, close-knit community, people living in a modern nation must make the cognitive leap that their identity is closely tied to that of a large number of people whom they have never met. Preconditions for the emergence of imagined communities include: world exploration; the growth of standardized time through the use of clocks and calendars; and, most significantly for Anderson, the spread of standardized languages through the print media. This last development implied a dramatic decline in global linguistic diversity but also allowed for people from relatively vast geographic regions to understand one another.

Since Anderson's initial work on nationalism, others have applied his ideas to different forms of group affiliation.[2] Research in this area focuses on the ways large-scale group identities are created and sustained symbolically in particular times and places. Special emphasis is usually given to the way individuals use these identities to interpret everyday life.

To say that an ethnic group constitutes an imagined community is not to say that it is false or somehow lacking in legitimacy. Rather, the imagined framework draws our attention to the symbolic nature of ethnicity, which may be meaningfully perpetuated even as seemingly intrinsic cultural characteristics are transformed through social and historical circumstances. Anderson argues, "Communities are to be distinguished, not by their falsity/genuineness, but by the style in which they are imagined."[3]

In this chapter we will explore how middle-class third-plus-generation Mexican Americans are able to perpetuate Mexican ethnicity within the relatively integrated environments they inhabit in and around Phoenix and San Jose. By using an "imaginary" approach in this analysis, I have deliberately chosen to downplay thinking about culture as a set of "traits" or fixed characteristics that define a cultural subgroup. Instead, I focus on how the people I spoke with utilize available cultural resources—specifically, Spanish-language television, Mexican food, religion, language, and gender roles—to reinforce and recreate Mexican ethnicity in their day-to-day lives.

On the whole, I am in agreement with Anderson and other social theorists who argue that "mediated experience," a defining characteristic of modern life, allows culture to be uprooted from its origins in local communities and interpersonal relations.[4] However, the third-plus-generation Mexican Americans I spoke with indicated that much of their exposure to Mexican culture is still tied to direct relationships with other members of the Mexican American community. That is, mestizaje in the United States, not unlike mestizaje in Mexico and other parts of Latin America, appears to consist of a complex mixture of both symbolic and relational elements.

My approach in this chapter is thus to sketch the range of cultural resources available, from relatively "unmediated" resources acquired through direct relationships and interactions with fellow Mexican Americans, to relatively mediated ones that may be acquired through television, radio, or commercial consumption, which do not require interacting with other members of the ethnic community. Interview responses suggest the entire range of cultural resources is used by third-plus-generation Mexican Americans at the individual level to produce Mexican ethnicity, though social integration and generations spent in the United States tend to favor the use of mediated over unmediated forms.

"Real" Mexican Food and "Bad" Mexican Ethnics

One of the cultural resources used by the people I spoke with to delineate their ethnicity is Mexican food. Though it is not my objective here to verify cultural authenticity, it was clear from their comments that many of the respondents held Mexican food to a high authentic standard. Quite a few remarked, for example, that they would not go out to eat Mexican food since many restaurants did not serve "real" Mexican food. In this regard, Michael, a manager in the regional office of a mortgage investment firm in Phoenix, says: "We still have the traditional meals, the traditional tamales and menudo, but we would never go out to eat Mexican. If we go out to eat it would probably be for other types of food."

Others would admit to going out for Mexican food, but only if it were served at an authentic Mexican restaurant, which usually meant it was owned and run by Mexican proprietors and catered primarily to a Mexican clientele. Fast food would definitely be out of the question. For Ken, however, a financial analyst in the San Francisco Bay area who had worked for a few months in Mexico City, the greatest derision was held for so-called upscale ethnic restaurants.

> Ken: I was talking to my boss and we're going to go to this Mexican food restaurant next week because one of my coworkers is leaving. And she's like, I want to go to Maya. And I'm like, what's that? It's high-end Mexican, she said. And I'm like, what's *that*? You get the best burritos in town? She's like, it's more of what an affluent Mexican would eat, say, like in Mexico City. And I'm like, what is THAT?!? [laughs]. Because the more affluent people in Mexico City, okay, they'll go and like they'll have steaks, or they'll go to a good Italian restaurant. I mean, have you ever been to Mexico City? And so I look at the menu, and it's the same old thing, typical beans and rice, but it will be neat flavored with some foo-foo lime sauce, or whatever. You know, it's all the same, it's just high-priced Mexican food.

Among the respondents, high-priced menus and fancy presentation were no substitute for an authentic Mexican food experience. Instead, those who did enjoy eating Mexican food out were much more likely to praise a local *taquería* or Mexican food stand that sold "real" Mexican food, made by Mexicans, at a reasonable price.

For others like Trina, a working mother of two in her mid-thirties, eating and preparing certain types of food at home are essential elements of being Mexican American, even if this means reinforcing certain ethnic stereotypes: "If you ask my son what's one of your favorite things to eat, he'll say a *burrito de frijoles*. You know that stereotype that Mexicans eat beans? Well, there's something to be said about that stereotype. We do eat a lot of beans. I mean we were raised eating beans."

Even when ethnic expectations with regard to food were not adhered to, it was still acknowledged that certain types of food were strongly tied to Mexican ethnicity. Sylvia, a single mother living in Mesa, Arizona, asserted: "I hate beans [laughs]. I don't make a good Mexican. I seldom make beans, but my kids love it. They have to go to nana's house to get beans. I've tried to make them, but I'm just not one of those people who likes to make beans. It's kind of a joke."

Thus, what is perceived as being an essential Mexican behavior is maintained as such simply by declaring that those who do not follow the pattern are not being "good" ethnics. The authentic ideal is maintained even after the actual practice has been abandoned.

It is notable that third-plus-generation Mexican Americans in the study were likely to focus on food as an important measure of their own ethnic authenticity, especially since Mexican food is one cultural resource to which the rest of the U.S. population has ready access. As opposed to other culturally specific resources, such as language and Spanish-language media, I believe the third-plus-generation Mexican Americans I spoke with were likely to point to food as a gauge of authenticity because this is, comparatively, the area in which they have the most experience. Of course, thanks to Mexican restaurants and ethnic food aisles in grocery stores across the country, Mexican food is also the way the rest of America has the most experience with Mexican culture. These mediated sources of ethnic fare thus serve to make the respondents' relational, authentic knowledge of it all the more crucial as a way of differentiating themselves from non-ethnics.

Mexican Catholicism

Another area where the notion of being a "bad" ethnic arose with some frequency was religion. Of the fifty people interviewed, twenty-eight claimed to be practicing Catholics who attended religious services with some regularity, twelve said they were raised Catholic but no longer practiced the religion, five identified simply as Christian, two as Presbyterian, and one each as Buddhist, atheist, and agnostic. Most of the practicing Catholics I spoke with were likely to make a strong connection between their religion and Mexican ethnicity. However, not unlike when they spoke about food, religion was an area where many respondents were able to recognize a central cultural trait (Catholicism), acknowledge their noncompliance, and yet maintain their ethnic affiliation simply by admitting they do not live up to the ideal. Ken, who was raised Catholic, observed: "If I was a good Mexican, I'd be Catholic right now. However, I must be a bad Mexican, because I'm not Catholic. I don't think religion plays a role in my life. I know it plays a role in my mom's life, and I know on my mom's side of the family the role it plays. But organized religion in my eyes has no place in my life."

Other "bad Mexicans" were less adamant about their rejection of Catholicism and were able to incorporate certain elements of the religion into their modern lives. Henry, a San Jose lawyer, pointed out that this was especially true when it complemented significant contemporary rituals, such as funerals, weddings, and professional rites of passage.

Henry: I'm what you call a bad Catholic, but I'm definitely a Catholic. I'm definitely a cultural Catholic—funerals, weddings, that sort of thing. And I have been divorced. But I think especially with Mexican Americans, it's a critical part of the culture, and it's hard to avoid. I mean my grandmother had a million St. Judes, you know, the patron saint of hopeless causes. And her grandmother was a *curandera*. I remember when I took the bar exam I was nervous because it's a hard test, and if I don't pass I might not keep my job, that sort of thing. And I went to my grandmother and I said, grandma, I'm very nervous about this test, what should I do? Without blinking she looked at me and she gave me a St. Jude statue. And she said, take St. Jude, wrap him in a towel and look at him and say, listen, I'm going to put you in this drawer and I'm not going to let you out until you help me pass the bar. And when you help me, then I'll give money to your church or hospital. And I said, okay. So I did it and I wrapped him up and six months later I got my results and I took him out after I had passed, and I said, thank you St. Jude. And I went to my grandmother and said, okay, what do I do now? And she said, give a hundred dollars to the hospital, and I said, for how long? And she said, you just do it every year, forever. And I said, that's a long time. So, now I give the money to St. Jude every year in her name at Christmas.

As Henry's comments make clear, religion is in large part something passed on from older to younger generations, making it very much a relational resource. It is, however, also apparent that religion is something the respondents felt they have a degree of control over as adults, whether they accept Catholicism, reject it, or decide to take up a completely different religion altogether. Ken's rejection of "organized religion" provides a good example of this. The willingness to take personal credit for generational changes in religious practice contrasts, as we shall see below, with the tendency to fault parents for not passing on Spanish-language skills to their children. As was the case with Mexican food, the perception that people have conscious control over religious practice was also evident in the way respondents lightheartedly referred to themselves as "bad" ethnics when they did not comply with religious expectations.

A Change for the Better:
Traditional Gender Roles and Mexican Culture

More so than was the case for religion, traditional gender roles were de-scribed by many respondents as a specific Mexican cultural trait, which they rejected. Mayra is a production scheduler for a Phoenix-area tech-nology firm who is currently married to a half-Mexican/half-Anglo man. By her account, the perceived treatment of women in Mexican culture affected her earlier preferences for dating:

> I never dated any Mexican guys except for one because the Mexican guys that I did know, I didn't like the way they treated their girlfriends. It wasn't how I wanted to be treated. The one guy that I did date in col-lege, asked me to sew a button on his shirt, and that was the last time I ever saw him. I'm like, you know what? I don't sew my own buttons on my clothes. Get out of here.

Mario, a community college student in his mid-twenties who plans to earn a bachelor's degree in accounting, talked about his reluctance to date Mexican-origin women because of traditional expectations about marriage and family, which he felt might conflict with his career plans:

> I don't think I want to be just married and have kids. I want a career. I don't want to be with someone who just wants to stay at home and raise kids. I don't think I want that, you know. I'm not too sure I even want kids. So, I know where I'm going, and now what I'm looking for is someone to help me to get to where I'm going, you know what I mean?

In contrast to their responses about food and religion, when respon-dents spoke about their rejection of traditional gender roles and expecta-tions in Mexican culture, they did not attempt to explain this break with tradition as an example of being a "bad" Mexican. Instead, most of the respondents who raised this issue conveyed a sense of optimism that a change in traditional gender roles, though at times difficult for the older generation to accept, was for the better. Cara, who left a Mexican Ameri-can community in Los Angeles to attend college in the San Francisco Bay area, spoke about how her mother has had to adjust to her daughter's new life away from home.

> Cara: I know she's proud of me, but actually she just threw it out there again the other day. I was talking about one of my friends getting mar-

ried, and we're like all across the country, and I'm a bridesmaid. And we're trying to plan the wedding, and of course we're doing it on the Internet because no one can get together in person. So, she's like, well, I hope you don't do that when you're getting married, try to plan it over the internet. That seems like so much hassle. See, if you would have stayed home, your bridesmaids could have been . . . , and then she starts naming all these girls in the neighborhood who I went to high school with. And she's like, that's why girls don't go away to college. And we both laughed. I mean, she just says it to irritate me. But I know she's very proud, I mean, I know I'm doing all these things that she probably would never do, and has never done. I know that sometimes she sees that, yeah, it's good—the freedom and going away—but then there's like all these ideas, and dating black guys, and not going to church. It's like I'm falling off the wayside [laughs]. But I think she's coming from what she's known. You know, she knows her environment, and it's comfortable, and it makes sense, and when you're not challenged, and you never go away, you never get to see the other things that are out there, that there are other ways that are right.

Traditional gender roles and expectations are an illustrative example of a primarily relational cultural resource. Among the people I spoke with, their understanding of traditional gender roles was mostly based on their interactions with Mexican American friends, family, and romantic relations. Not surprisingly, given the respondents' educational background and professional status, traditional gender roles were the cultural resource most readily rejected among those who chose to talk about it. Whereas many of the respondents admitted a tinge of ethnic guilt for not practicing Catholicism, or not liking or knowing how to prepare certain ethnic foods, no one I spoke with openly regretted cross-generational changes in expected gender roles.

The Meaning of an Unspoken Language

Of all the cultural resources the respondents spoke about in their interviews, none appeared to be more associated in their minds with Mexican ethnicity than the Spanish language. This was remarkable since the vast majority of them did not speak it. Forty-three of the fifty respondents were raised speaking primarily English, four were raised speaking primarily Spanish, and three speaking a mix of the two idioms. For those who did speak Spanish, the acquisition of the language was often connected directly to the presence of a family member who spoke primarily Spanish. In this regard, a Spanish-speaking grandparent could have varying effects on the language ability of siblings in the same family. Phil, a Phoenix-area marketing manager, observed:

> When my grandparents were alive, I could only speak Spanish, and they died when I was pretty young, about eight years old. When they died my need for Spanish went out the window. Everybody else around me spoke English. My brothers, they were older when my grandparents died, so their retention of Spanish was much better than mine. Their command of the language is much better. In fact, my one brother is a police officer down in Mesa, and he's a translator down there. He does interviews and interrogations in Spanish and he has great Spanish, whereas I struggle with it. You know, I can speak it, but it's very choppy, and broken, and, you know, *pocho*.

Phil's account of his relationship with his grandparents, as well as that of his brother's work as a police officer, draws attention to the rather obvious point that Spanish-language ability is very closely tied to the opportunity to speak it. Of the seven third-plus-generation people in the interview sample who still speak Spanish as adults, all of them either use the language regularly as part of their work, or they speak it at home with Spanish-speaking family members, and, in some cases, a little of both.

The overwhelming majority of the people in the sample, however, do not speak Spanish in their day-to-day lives. Claudia, an administrator in a non-profit organization, summed up a common sentiment of loss among many of the respondents with regard to Spanish-language ability and ambivalence towards their parents for not passing this key cultural attribute onto their children:

> I would get mad at [my parents] as I got older, you know. Why didn't you just teach us Spanish? And, their answer was, well, we had a hard time when we grew up, so we thought we would make it easier for our children. [Pause] But there is a loss there. You know, I do really get upset with my parents, but I don't blame them and I understand where they were coming from. Somehow some families are able to do both English and Spanish, but it wasn't the case in my family.

The centrality of language for Mexican-origin identity was evident in the strong emotional response a few of the people I interviewed expressed when talking about what they felt was a lost opportunity to speak Spanish. David, a computer-programming student from Scottsdale, makes a direct connection between language loss and a deliberate strategy of assimilation on the part of his father.

TM: Did [your father] try to teach you Spanish?

David: No, never did. There's a huge story behind that. It's this thing where both of my dad's wives were Anglo. My mother was Anglo, my stepmother is Anglo. And, I think that my dad growing up in all the prejudice in Dallas was made to feel so bad. . . . If you'll pardon me for a second [He stops to wipe his eyes]. He, uh, yeah, he wanted his children to be Anglo. So, we didn't learn Spanish. How could he see . . . ? [Pause] There's some paradox in that. He was working in the Chicano Movement, but at the same time he was like, well, the movement is one thing, we'll do what we can, but at the same time he would prefer that his children just didn't have to put up with any of this shit. So, he wanted his children to be as Anglicized as possible so that we could move as white men in a white man's world.

David's account is particularly poignant in the way it captures the central tension of culture and language many Mexican Americans, including seasoned activists, carry with them. The Chicano Movement in particular saw the retention of Mexican culture as an essential tool in the fight against Anglo domination. At the same time, one could not raise a child without considering the individual-level disadvantages of cultural discrimination imposed by those in power. In that sense, many Chicanos and Chicanas found themselves in a position not very different from that of their World War II–generation parents when it came to raising their own children.

Other respondents were more matter-of-fact than David about their lack of Spanish skills. For those who grew up in an English-dominant social context, parents would occasionally, if unintentionally, provide negative associations with the Spanish language. Ted, a San Francisco Bay area accountant, argues this point below.

Ted: When my parents didn't want us to know what they were saying, they'd speak Spanish. They actually tried to get us to speak some Spanish and stuff. But we were given a choice, and as kids when you're given a choice, you'll always take the easy way out.

TM: Did they talk about what language you should use?

Ted: It wasn't like they talked about it. But when they spoke Spanish, nine times out of ten they would be telling you to do chores. It wasn't like they were telling you pleasant things. You know, if you're trying to tell me you're going to give me some ice cream, then I think I'd try to learn that language pretty quick. But, generally when mom and dad spoke it, they were going back and forth talking about all the screw-ups you did for the day and you were about to get in trouble. So, from my perspective, as kids there just wasn't much of an incentive to learn it.

The parent-child dynamic described by Ted is, in fact, quite mundane. At some point, Spanish becomes the language of social control by parents who wish to keep information away from their English-speaking children. And then, to make matters worse, as emotions rise and sternness is required, Spanish also becomes the language of discipline, a way of demarcating the seriousness of doing household chores or getting along with siblings. As Ted's comments suggest, these are not the kinds of things that tend to endear children to their parents' language.

Beyond simply accepting their linguistic fate, others were quite satisfied with their parents' decision to raise them speaking mainly English. As Dan, the aspiring mariachi quoted at the beginning of this chapter, observed of his childhood:

I give a lot of credit to my dad for where I'm at now. He understood that he needed to give me the best opportunity to succeed, and that included speaking in English well, being able to articulate what you want to say, and just providing me with those tools. Spanish, he really didn't place much emphasis on that at the time. Now, I think he would actually prefer that I be able to speak Spanish because, as anyone knows, it's an invaluable asset.

Dan's reflection on his father's choice to teach him English as a child draws our attention to the complicated role Spanish plays in the lives of third-plus-generation Mexican Americans, a role that terms like "linguistic assimilation" or, to borrow a rougher term from the Chicano Movement, "vendido" (cultural sellout), do not adequately capture. Like traditional gender roles, Spanish-language knowledge was a very relational cultural resource in the lives of the people I interviewed, grounded in the day-to-day acquisition of this knowledge through interaction with family members.

Instead of rejecting this resource, however, as was the case with traditional gender roles, the most common sentiment expressed among the
interviewees with regard to Spanish was one of loss. If a few of the respondents did grow up speaking at least some Spanish, the relational aspect
of Spanish for most of the respondents was, more often than not, that of
their parents not speaking it to them, or occasionally using the language in
such a way so as to discourage their children from wanting to learn it. The
explanations for this provided by the parents usually centered on making
life easier for their children in the English-dominant United States and trying to protect them from the language-based discrimination many of them
experienced when they were growing up. The respondents' attitudes in
the face of this loss ranged from ambivalent feelings of anger mixed with
sympathy towards their parents for denying them an opportunity, to being
quite satisfied with their parents' choice to teach their children mainly
English.

The rather pragmatic belief expressed by Dan that Spanish could serve
as an "invaluable asset" was shared by many of the Mexican American professionals I spoke with and contributed to the sense of regret among some
of the respondents that they did not learn the language in childhood. It is
thus perhaps not surprising that the majority of the respondents who did
not grow up speaking Spanish made efforts to learn it later in life by taking
courses in high school or college and/or spending time abroad in Mexico
or Spain. It is to these experiences across culture and space that we turn
to in the next section.

Language and Cross-National Encounters

For Joe, a public relations professional working in San Jose, a trip to Mexico while he was still in college proved to be a transformative experience
that led to further efforts to improve his Spanish skills and knowledge of
Mexican culture. Early on in the interview he told me that he had through
much of his youth downplayed his Mexican ethnicity, going so far as to tell
some of his high school friends he was actually Italian. I asked him when it
was that he came to accept his Mexican heritage. His response follows.

> It literally started overnight. It was during the latter part of college that
> I went to Mexico with my parents, Puerto Vallarta, you know, some-
> thing really touristy. But one day they went off to do some fishing trip
> or something, and I walked around, and I found myself in old town,
> which is not touristy, which is very authentic Mexico, and I wound up

talking to this old man in the church courtyard. And even with my broken Spanish we understood each other. He was telling me about what it was like to live in Mexico, and its history, and this and that, and I just got fascinated by it. And I just started to think, I want to learn more. So, I took something from that trip back here. I wanted to do things, and it was like, wow, I could start taking Spanish classes. I want to study Mexican American culture. You know, all of the sudden my bookcase is just full of books by Mexican American authors, and it's all because of this trip.

By Joe's account, his vacation in Mexico turned into nothing short of an ethnic epiphany. A few of the Mexican Americans I spoke with, however, had considerably less momentous encounters with Mexican nationals while traveling in Mexico. For example, I asked Carolyn, a bank teller in San Jose, if she had ever spent much time in Mexico.

Carolyn: On vacation, yes. We go to Puerto Vallarta, Cabo, Tijuana, you know, Mazatlan.

TM: Do you interact much with people when you're down there?

Carolyn: Yeah, I talk to them. But, they don't appreciate it. They're offended. They're insulted, I should say, by the fact that I am *Mexicana* and I do not speak Spanish. They get angry. And, it's like, hey! I'm one of you guys. That's one of those things where I think we don't stick together. They take offense by the fact that I do not speak Spanish fluently.

Even within the United States, the lack of Spanish language ability among the third-plus-generation Mexican Americans can occasionally lead to unpleasant interactions with Mexican nationals. Leo, an airline attendant living in Phoenix, made it clear, however, that many Mexican Americans are likely to attribute this kind of unpleasantness more to the rudeness of specific individuals than to their own lack of fluency in Spanish.

Leo: I had this weird experience about eight years ago coming out of Tucson. I had two Hispanic people, they were from Mexico, and they started speaking in Spanish and I told them, you know, I don't speak it so well, but she wanted to know what time we arrived. And she was going to Ontario, like Tucson-Phoenix-Ontario, and I told her the time we were arriving in Phoenix. And she shook her head and I heard her saying in Spanish, look at this dumb Mexican, doesn't speak Spanish.

What kind of dumb Mexicans do they have working here? And I turned around and I said, I may not speak Spanish, but at least I speak some Spanish and a lot of English. You only speak Spanish. And she got real embarrassed.

Fortunately, most cross-national encounters described by the respondents were not so acrimonious. This is indeed fortunate since the proximity to Mexico and ongoing immigration mean interactions with Spanish-speaking Mexican nationals in the Southwest and California are common among the third-plus generation. The contrasting ways in which language is used during these encounters—as a marker of cultural difference within the Mexican-origin population or a bridge across immigrant generations—profoundly colors the ways third-plus-generation individuals imagine their own Mexican ethnicity. A pleasant encounter, such as Joe's in Puerto Vallarta, can lead to a newfound interest in Mexico, its culture, and its people. In contrast, unfriendly encounters, such as those experienced by Carolyn and Leo, may cause one to question just how strong cross-national bonds actually are.

For the most part, cross-generational interactions described by the respondents were friendly and seen as inevitable facts of life in places like Phoenix and San Jose, where first-generation Mexican immigrants constitute a large portion of the regional working class. Susan, a Phoenix-area accountant in her early thirties, pointed out:

Just being a homeowner, there are a lot of Mexican workers who do that kind of work. So, like I had a block wall put in, and one guy came out here and there were two other guys working with him and they didn't speak any English. And at first it was kind of frustrating because I can't make them understand me and I don't understand them. And it's like, I'm going to need to get used to that because, you know, they're willing to do the work and they're doing a good job and, you know, we'll find a way to communicate.

In all, four of the respondents had regular contact with Mexican immigrants at work; two of the respondents were married to first-generation immigrants; and quite a few still have living grandparents who are themselves immigrants. Mexican immigration for third-plus-generation Mexican Americans is, thus, not a romantic place in the ethnic past longed for in the present, but rather an ongoing fact of everyday life. For the people I spoke with, this means maintaining actual relationships with people from Mexico and coming face-to-face with cross-national differences in language, culture, and class that third-plus-generation European Americans have rarely had to confront.

Spanish-Language Media

An additional everyday reminder of ethnic origins directly tied to the growing size of the Spanish-speaking population is Spanish-language television, watched in nearly half (twenty-three out of fifty) of the respondents' homes. Often, respondents like Margaret, an administrative assistant working in San Jose, justified watching Spanish-language television to improve their Spanish-language ability:

> Sometimes I watch the novellas [Spanish-language soap operas] just so I can try to pick up on the Spanish. Because my grandma, she can speak and understand English but she likes to speak Spanish. So, she'll speak to me and I'll try to respond, and she'll say, *ay, mijita*, I keep on forgetting that your Spanish is not that good. But, she still speaks to me in Spanish. So, I do watch the novellas just to kind of help me learn something, and I do.

Many respondents tied their Spanish-language viewing to their relationship with Spanish-speaking relatives. Vicki, a Phoenix-area high school math teacher, noted that her grandmother often helps as an interpreter when she watches Spanish-language television: "I go and visit my grandmother every Thursday and I watch the Spanish soap operas. There's a lot I don't get, but she'll explain everything to me. If I were watching alone, I'd have trouble, but with her and the little I know I'm able to piece it together."

In addition to watching television, many of the respondents said they listened to Spanish-language radio and Latin music originating from both Mexico and other parts of Latin America. The growing recognition among corporate America and media outlets over the past decade of the size of the burgeoning "Hispanic market" within the United States means that Americans, in general, are much more likely to be exposed to Spanish-language media than they have been in the past. While other Americans may also take advantage of Spanish-language radio, television, and newspapers to hone their language skills and gain access to this mediated aspect of Latin culture, third-plus-generation Latinos, such as the Mexican Americans I spoke with, have the privilege of linking this access to their ethnic heritage.

Mexican Ethnicity across Generations: Is It "Real" or Is It Mediated?

The way Spanish-language television is used to produce Mexican ethnicity presents perhaps the most obvious opportunity to apply Anderson's notion of the imagined community to the Mexican American experience. Without actually knowing most of its members, Spanish-language television allows third-plus-generation Mexican Americans to imagine themselves as part of a broad ethnic collectivity. A recent critique of the "Hispanic media," however, casts doubt on the explanatory power of the imagined community approach in this regard. In their efforts to convince advertisers that Latinos constitute one homogeneous market in the United States, Arlene Davila argues, Hispanic ad firms have tended to downplay generational, class, and national-origin differences among Latinos.[5] National Spanish-language television networks, in turn, provide "Latino programming" across the United States, such that Mexican American viewers like Margaret and Vicki may work on improving their Spanish-language skills by watching Peruvian soap operas or talk and variety shows produced in Miami and hosted by people of Cuban, Chilean, and other Latin American origins.

Though Spanish-language television may be working to help create a "pan-ethnic" Latino ethnicity, the role it plays in producing a specifically Mexican-origin ethnicity is unclear.[6] If anything, the respondents' comments suggest Spanish-language television works to reinforce Mexican ethnicity only to the degree that a prior connection to Mexican ethnicity, grounded in actual relationships to other Mexican Americans, already exists.

That said, Spanish-language television does have the "imagined" quality of granting interested individuals access to "Latino culture" without requiring them to actually interact with other Latinos. I would argue that it is precisely the indiscriminate access to this cultural resource that gives it its imagined quality. One may watch Spanish-language television to maintain a cultural bond with one's Mexican American grandmother, or one may watch it because, as an Anglo living in California, it would be interesting to learn something about Latino culture or practice Spanish comprehension.

Likewise, if we return to Dan's quote at the beginning of this chapter, though it is clear that he imbues the ability to play the mariachi trumpet with specific ethnic meaning that would tie him to his Mexican American heritage, this does not preclude the possibility of a non–Mexican American learning to play just as well or better and without the accompanying ethnic sentiment. In both cases, mediated culture—in the first instance through television and in the second through the cultural institution where Dan takes his lessons—provides open access to cultural knowledge for anyone interested in acquiring it.

By focusing in this chapter on cultural resources, as opposed to intrinsic cultural traits, I have attempted to draw attention to the meaningful social context within which culture is understood and utilized by the respondents to reinforce and recreate their Mexican ethnicity. In this regard, I have extrapolated from Anderson's conceptualization of the "imagined community" to argue that cultural resources may be thought of as a continuum that ranges from being primarily unmediated and grounded in actual relationships with co-ethnics, to primarily mediated through television, radio, and cultural institutions that permit open access to cultural resources to all, regardless of ethnicity. Using this scale, and based on the interview data, I would tentatively rank the cultural resources discussed in this chapter from most unmediated to most mediated in the following order: traditional gender relations, language, religion, Mexican food, and Spanish-language television.

It is perhaps not surprising that cultural resources on the unmediated side of the scale, those most strongly based on interactions with members of the Mexican-origin population, are those most likely to be lost as Mexican Americans become integrated into U.S. society. The contrasting attitudes in the face of these losses are noteworthy. In the case of traditional gender roles, respondents appeared content to leave behind gender expectations deemed to be more restrictive than those encountered in the dominant society; whereas with language, many respondents expressed a good deal of regret for not having learned Spanish in their youth. It is possible that the respondents' high average educational attainment affects their expressed devaluation of traditional gender relations and positive valuation of language skills. That is, it may be their relatively privileged position that allows them to perceive firsthand both the material benefits of granting women more freedom in their lifestyles and career choices, and the social and professional advantages of speaking Spanish well.

Though the manner in which respondents spoke about language was similar to the way they spoke about gender relations, in that much of their talk centered on relationships, their insight into Spanish-language loss and acquisition also suggested some mediated elements. The attempts on the part of most of the English-dominant respondents to improve their Spanish language ability through courses or traveling have an imagined quality to them since, again, they represent opportunities at acquiring cultural knowledge that are open to anyone. It is only the meaning that third-plus-generation Mexican Americans give these experiences that allows them to reinforce or produce their Mexican ethnicity.

Spanish-language television and Mexican food present more obvious examples of mediated cultural resources in American society. One could make use of these resources without having to interact with another human being. This is, of course, not the way most third-plus-generation respondents experienced them. Instead, even something as obviously mediated as Spanish-language television was often connected to the respondents' lives through their relationships with Spanish-speaking relatives who served as either interpreters or inspiration to improve Spanish comprehension. And, in the case of Mexican food, unmediated ethnic experience was used as a guard against threats to authenticity presented by the commercial fare offered at mainstream or upscale Mexican restaurants.

Religion, I propose, lies somewhere in the middle—though it is in a sense mediated through religious institutions, its unmediated content passed down through generations of families makes it ethnically significant. Third-plus-generation Mexican Americans are able to play with this dual nature when they make claim to being "culturally Catholic" or when they, noting their lack of religious adherence, refer to themselves as "bad" ethnics. They can, if they choose, reject or modify religion as mediated by religious institutions without having to feel they have somehow compromised their ethnicity.

In sum, the study of ethnic culture since the mid–twentieth century has made considerable advances, not the least of which has been the recognition that culture is not adequately understood as a fixed set of essential traits that may be used to differentiate one group from another or to judge levels of assimilation among individuals within the same group. Instead, works such as *Imagined Communities* have encouraged us to look at the ways culture and identity are actively created and recreated with the resources at hand in specific times and places. In this chapter, I have looked at the way third-plus-generation Mexican Americans in the present day use both mediated and unmediated cultural resources to produce Mexican ethnicity. This study suggests predominantly mediated cultural resources are those most likely to be utilized by this highly integrated subgroup of the Mexican-origin population to perpetuate Mexican ethnicity. It is still, however, the unmediated, relational connection to the Mexican American community that endows these mediated experiences with ethnic meaning. As we shall see in the next chapter, one important way of maintaining connections to this community is through membership in ethnic identity organizations.

3 Work, Organizations, and the Legacy of Chicanismo

In this book, I would like to add some flesh to the bones of mestizaje. I would prefer mestizaje served as more than a metaphor applied broadly to any instance of cultural hybridity or borderland experience. One point I would like to begin to make in this chapter is that mestizaje is not primarily a choice. Though, as was made clear in the previous chapter, individuals actively participate in the construction of Mexican American ethnicity, a fundamental aspect of American Mestizaje is that it is profoundly structured by U.S. political history and the demographic present of the American Southwest.

In this regard, a primary force shaping American Mestizaje over the last forty years has been identity-based activism, which reached its zenith in the late 1960s and early 1970s. One result of the Civil Rights Movement, the Chicano Movement, and other minority group activism of that period was the transformation of the meaning of racial and ethnic identity, turning what was once considered a marginal status outside the American mainstream into a matter of group pride.[1] Among the third-plus-generation Mexican Americans interviewed for this study in 2001, the legacy of that earlier era was evident in both the kind of voluntary work they participated in and the way in which they interpreted the professional work setting, where there was usually a notable lack of fellow ethnics and other people of color.

In this chapter I examine Mexican ethnicity among third-plus-generation professionals at the workplace and through participation in voluntary organizations. I argue that changes related to the emergence of identity politics in the 1960s have meant entry into society's mainstream institutions of business and government no longer requires the exchange of ethnic for professional identities. To the contrary, ethnic identity professional organizations have emerged as a key source of ethnic networking for Mexican American professionals who typically find themselves in work settings with low levels of minority representation.

Following a brief overview of the sociological debates concerning structural assimilation, this chapter is broken into two major sections, the first concerning Mexican American participation in voluntary organizations and the second concerning Mexican ethnicity in the workplace.

Voluntary Organizations, Work, and Structural Assimilation

In *Assimilation in American Life,* Gordon (1964) argues that cultural differences in language, lifestyles, and religious practice, despite being the most obvious and, for the xenophobic, most disturbing characteristics of new groups in American society, were also the aspects of ethnic life most quick to change. Ethnic groups, especially by the second and third generation, readily assumed cultural patterns of the American mainstream. Their more serious challenge was that of structural assimilation, that is, the establishment of "primary," personal relationships with members of the dominant society, indicated by "large-scale entrance into the cliques, clubs, and institutions" of the "host society."[2] The descendants of immigrants, Gordon asserted, were much more likely to develop their own parallel institutions within the ethnic community than be admitted into the mainstream.

Gordon's original account of parallel institutions is largely descriptive, supporting his thesis that the primary mode of incorporation for ethnic groups in the United States was through "structural pluralism." This implied the existence of separate ethnic "subsocieties" in which voluntary organizations, social networks, and even commercial enterprises were preserved apart from mainstream American society.[3]

Social scientists studying immigrant groups and their descendants today, however, are likely to use the notion of parallel institutions in a normative fashion. In contrast to Gordon, they argue that the maintenance of dense social networks and institutions within ethnic communities is an effective strategy for protecting the native-born descendants of immigrants from poverty and the more deleterious aspects of American popular culture.[4] This view is supported by research that highlights the success of groups, such as the Sikhs in southern California and the Cuban Americans in Miami. These and other ethnic enclaves, where cultural practices and values are maintained within a tightly knit community context, facilitate economic advancement and represent a kind of "third way" out of the constraints of segmented assimilation.[5]

Both the classic definition of parallel institutions proposed by Gordon,

and the normative formulation of "selective acculturation" espoused by sociologists such as Alejandro Portes, stress the internal insular quality of
ethnic institutions and organizations. In Gordon's descriptive approach,
this form of ethnic separateness presents a challenge to democratic participation in American civic life. Through Portes' normative lens it provides
the communal framework within which the descendents of immigrants
can find the social and, indeed, psychological support needed to improve
their life chances in what is often an unfavorable socioeconomic context.
In stressing insularity, however, both approaches neglect the ways ethnic
institutions may directly facilitate structural assimilation.

I find some support in this chapter for the parallel institution and selective acculturation arguments, though not as strategies or processes occurring prior to and separate from structural assimilation. Rather, there
is evidence that ethnic forms of organization serve to facilitate direct integration into mainstream society by promoting ethnic camaraderie across
work settings in professions where Mexican Americans are greatly underrepresented. Moreover, these same organizations often maintain mentoring and other programs that foster awareness of the professions they represent among the younger generation in the predominantly working-class
Mexican-origin community.

Mexican American Participation in Voluntary Organizations

Before taking a closer look at the interviewees' perspective on voluntary
organizations, it is worth recalling the rich history of Mexican American
participation in voluntary associations, such as the Alianza Hispano-
Americana, the League of United Latin American Citizens (LULAC), and the
G.I. Forum. The earliest of these groups, the Alianza Hispano-Americana,
was established in Tucson, Arizona, in 1894 as a basis for Mexican ethnic solidarity in the face of Anglo political dominance and discrimination.
As political historian David Gutierrez argues, the Alianza was notable
in its time for the degree of unity it promoted between immigrants and
U.S.–born Mexican Americans.[6] As Alianza members, recent immigrants
entered a welcoming environment where they were introduced to American culture and politics in a non-threatening fashion. And it appears class
solidarity may have been every bit as important as ethnic identity in Mexican American organizations such as Alianza at the turn of the nineteenth
century. Though Gutierrez acknowledges that much of the leadership of

these early groups came from middle-class backgrounds, the bulk of their rank and file consisted of low-wage laborers.[7]

LULAC, founded in Corpus Christi, Texas, in 1929, shared Alianza's vision of fighting discrimination against Mexican Americans, and by the post-war period it had established itself as a key player in the struggle for civil rights. In supporting a series of legal challenges against Texas school districts that maintained "separate-but-equal" policies for Mexican American and Anglo children, LULAC helped lay the groundwork for the 1954 Supreme Court decision in *Brown v. Board of Education* against *de jure* segregation.[8]

Membership in LULAC, and later in the veteran-based G.I. Forum, was made up disproportionately of the emerging Mexican American middle class. In contrast to the Alianza Hispano-Americana, membership in these later groups consisted almost entirely of U.S.–born citizens. Perhaps not surprisingly, the political approach of these two organizations reflected the middle-class striving of their members with particular emphasis given to their rights as American citizens and their productive contribution to American society. The organizational transformation of LULAC in the 1970s and 1980s has been well documented. Political scientist Benjamin Marquez has argued that changes in the organization's incentive structure and increased reliance on outside funding ultimately severed it from its community-based activist roots.[9]

The rise to prominence of the Chicano Movement in the 1960s and 1970s marked a sea change in the symbolic imagination of Mexican American politics. The older generation's ideal of integration and mainstream assimilation was jettisoned in favor of the politics of cultural pride and, for the more radically inclined, ethnic nationalism. Ignacio Garcia argues that, today, the activism of the Chicano Movement, now long past its apex of the early 1970s, continues to play an important symbolic role in maintaining a link between the Mexican American middle class and the working-class community. Thus, though many of the *movimiento*'s more nationalist goals may have failed, the "Chicano ethos" still remains. The Chicano ethos, according to Garcia, does not see ethnic consciousness and social integration with mainstream America as contradictory tendencies.[10] And as will be shown in this chapter, one need not even self-identify as Chicano or Chicana to demonstrate outward signs of Chicano consciousness.

Organizations and Mexican Ethnicity

The thirty-six people interviewed who were actively involved in voluntary associations participated in a total of twenty-six professional and twenty non-professional organizations. Not surprisingly, given the sample selection process, the two most popular professional organizations among the interviewees were a Hispanic business professional organization, of which seven were members, and a Hispanic engineering organization, of which five were members. Both of these organizations were my initial starting point for sampling in the San Jose area. An association for Latinos working in the media was the third most common professional organization, indicated by three of the Phoenix-area respondents. Other professional organizations the respondents participated in included the California Bar Association, the Hispanic Chamber of Commerce, and a professional accounting association.

The most popular non-professional organizations, mentioned by four respondents, were those related to their children's interests. These included coaching, the Girl Scouts, and the Parent Teacher Association (PTA). Other examples of current volunteer activity, indicated by three respondents, included work done for local arts groups, church groups, mentoring organizations, and community development. Other non-professional organizations listed were Habitat for Humanity, the National Rifle Association, and Special Olympics.

Skateboarding Alone and Non-Participation

Despite the fact that the sample was initially drawn from people who were somehow associated with volunteer organizations or the non-profit sector, fourteen, or over a quarter of the fifty people interviewed, were not currently involved in volunteer work at all. In recent years, political scientist Robert Putnam has noted the declining participation among Americans in voluntary associations.[11] This trend is pointed to as an indicator of lower levels of civic engagement and "social capital." This last term refers to features of social life that tend to promote coordination, cooperation, and face-to-face communication. According to Putnam, these central features of social capital ultimately strengthen democracy and benefit society as a whole.

Reasons for the decline in voluntary participation include people having fewer children; longer hours spent at work; more time spent commuting; and the individualization of leisure time. The reasons given by the interviewees in this study for not participating in voluntary organizations in many ways parallel those given by Putnam. David, for example, the computer-programming student, explains his preference for associating with people on an individual basis rather than through organizations: "Growing up, you know, I was in the suburbs in the '80s and that's when punk rock hit. So, I was getting involved in that and skateboarding and it made me really shy away from organizations of any kind. I look for individuals, you know, I make friends with other people who are not involved in any institutionalized organizations."

A more common sentiment expressed by the interviewees was simply not having enough time to participate in the voluntary organizations they feel are important. As Mayra, a production scheduler for a technology firm in the Phoenix-area, points out, when it comes down to making a choice between doing volunteer work and spending time with family, family often wins out: "I would like to be involved in more things. Like in college I was involved in Habitat for Humanity, which I loved. But, I've just found that I'm too busy, the story of everyone's lives, I'm sure. But I'm trying to prioritize things right now and the one big thing that I'm trying to do is spend more time with my family." Like many Americans across categories of class and race, Mayra and a few other respondents in this study pointed to their own version of the "time bind" rooted in hours spent at work and with family as the reason for their lack of voluntary participation.

Volunteering for Children and Young Adults

For a few respondents, however, volunteer work and time with family are not mutually exclusive activities. To the contrary, for parents like Keith, the director of a university student outreach program, participation in volunteer work is directly tied to devoting time to their children's lives. As he notes, much of the volunteer work he does with his children also ends up benefiting the Latino community, though this is not his primary motive: "I volunteer to work at my church, I coach the girls' basketball team. I volunteer coaching little league soccer. I'm a volunteer umpire. They pay, well, a hot dog and a Coke. I do that in the Latino community but I don't seek out organizations and volunteering because of an ethnicity. I'll go because I'm trying to help. And if it happens to be a Latino community, all the more power to it."

Joe, on the other hand, who has worked in the past as a newspaper journalist and has no children of his own, feels it is important that the mentoring work he does with community college and high school students benefits the Mexican American and Latino community. As he observes,

> I'm just more involved in a lot more things related to the Latino community. I'm a mentor in a Latino-oriented program. I got involved with that primarily because I wanted to help out Mexican American kids. I initially got involved with it because I did a story on the project. They asked if I wanted to be a mentor and I said, sure. I did it first with college kids, and then later with the high schools.

Like Joe, many of the professionals I interviewed believed mentoring was an important way of sharing their experiences in higher education and in the professional workforce with Latino youth who otherwise might not have the opportunity. In the case of Lydia, a San Jose engineer in her mid-twenties, the mentoring work she has done with Latino high school students through a professional Hispanic engineering association represents a direct payback to the program that initially drew her to engineering when she was a teenager. After describing the mentoring work she does currently, she talked a bit about her experience in the same program as a student in high school.

> Lydia: There was a program at Fresno State that the local chapter put on to get minority students from Fresno into engineering programs. It was like a one-week extensive course, kind of like a camp, and we just learned about the different types of engineering, and we talked to a lot of different people and different corporations to see what kind of people they needed. And this was in high school, so it kind of got us thinking in the right way, where we should go to school and what we want to study. You really don't know what you want to do when you're in high school. I mean, you kind of know you want to get out of the house, but you don't know how. You know, your options are get out and get married, but how do you support yourself? And, college is like an intermediate step, but that's one thing Latino students just aren't aware of. So, it was a very eye-opening experience.

Intentionally or not, the relationships college-educated Mexican Americans foster through volunteer work serve as an important bridge for the younger generation. Given the low numbers of university graduates among Mexican Americans, every example of academic success provided by volunteers like Lydia is a welcome boost, increasing the chances that those next in line will strive for a university education. And college is where the cycle of voluntary participation often begins.

College Organizations

In addition to providing the people I interviewed with the education necessary to advance economically, college was also the time when many of them first became involved in volunteer associations, some ethnic identity-based and some not. Of the former category, there were two main types that people recalled: professional, usually "Hispanic" organizations that were intended to prepare students for their jobs after college, and MEChA (Movimiento Estudiantil Chicano de Aztlán), often described by the respondents as the more "radical" activist group on campus that worked for social justice issues on behalf of the Chicana/o community. For Eva, a single mother in her late twenties, MEChA was also an important way of integrating into college life at Northern Arizona University. As she puts it, "I just thought it was good because, being in [MEChA], you got to be with your people. You know, you get to express your concerns, you could relate, everybody understood what you were talking about. . . . It was really good for me."

Michael, however, a former officer in the Hispanic Business Students Association (HBSA) at Arizona State and currently an investment firm manager in Phoenix, felt the goals of MEChA and other more mainstream ethnic organizations on campus often clashed:

> The Mechistas were more concerned with civil rights, that kind of thing. They took on those types of issues, like schooling and whether or not we were being treated fairly, and whatever else the community was fighting for, which I'm not denigrating. It's important what they were doing. We supported those types of things, but we had a more a business-oriented organization, and there was friction between the two groups because they said, you guys are like the white people. And so there were people in MEChA who thought we were selling out to the corporate world.

Quite a few of the interviews brought up this basic contrast on college campuses between the more politically conservative "Hispanic" student groups and the more activist "Chicano" organizations. But as Henry, a San Jose lawyer, observes, the strict political lines drawn between groups in college become more difficult to maintain outside the university setting:

> If you weren't completely in agreement with the [MEChA] leadership, then basically they didn't want you. And that wasn't so much spoken as unspoken. And, as I've learned, that happens with a lot of Latino

groups, especially in college where there's a critical mass of Latinos to choose from and you can do that. Then when you get out in the work world, you know, here I work in this office with 220 attorneys and there are ten Latino attorneys, and only about six of them really admit it. And so, you can't really be as choosy as people were in college.

Advocacy and the "Chicano Ethos"

Much of what follows concerning Mexican Americans in the workplace confirms what Henry is saying—Mexican American professionals typically work in environments where there are not many other Latinos. That said, the ethos of the Chicano Movement that compels Mechistas and other Chicano activists to maintain their cultural and social ties to the working-class Mexican-origin community is also evident in the comments and actions of many of the college-educated professionals I interviewed. These are people who participate in volunteer work but may prefer to distance themselves from what they perceive as "radical" politics. Thus, though Michael was an officer in the relatively conservative HBSA and did not always see eye-to-eye with MEChA activists when he was in college, he is now an active member in a community development organization in the Phoenix area. This particular organization sees its mission as advocating not for the "Hispanic," or even for the "Mexican American," but rather for the "Chicano" community, in the areas of affordable housing and work-force training.

A post-college interest in supporting the working-class Mexican-origin community, through mentoring or some other form of volunteer work, was not uncommon among the people I spoke with. Phil, for example, a marketing manager at a Phoenix-area utility company, told me how he initially got interested in Chicanos por la Causa (CPLC) (the same group Michael volunteers for):

> Well, I read a little bit about them, and I thought, wow, these guys have an interesting little history. So, I contacted one of the board members and told him that I was interested. You know, when you look at [CPLC] in the '70s versus [CPLC] in the '90s, it's a different organization. Activism was very much a part of the movement, so a lot more advocacy took place. A lot more "in your face" kind of advocacy took place. I still think that should be taking place. And it is, but they're not as aggressive with it, in my opinion, as they should be.

Even if CPLC, in Phil's view, may not be living up to its more "aggressive" potential, it is this organization's history of activism within the Chicano community that drew him to it in the first place. Ignacio Garcia (1997) has argued that the Chicano Movement, not unlike the Mexican Revolution by which it was in part inspired, has become largely institutionalized into the mainstream of American politics. More radical undertakings, such as the establishment of a separatist Raza Unida party, were not fully realized. The Chicano ethos, however, still remains such that middle-class Mexican American professionals and activists alike maintain an interest in a politics of empowerment that emphasizes a strong ethnic identity and recognition of working-class roots. At the same time, Garcia argues, present-day Mexican Americans are unlikely to espouse the separatist rhetoric of the earlier movement.

This institutionalization explains, to some degree, Phil's disappointment with the present strategies of CPLC that do not match up with the organization's more confrontational history. It also helps us understand the way ethnicity, far from being a matter of private concern, has become very much a matter of public concern since the identity movements of the 1960s and 1970s.

The Convergence of Working-Class and Professional Identities

Most of the people I interviewed who were involved in volunteer work expressed a sense of obligation towards the Mexican-origin or Latino community. There appear to be three primary explanations for this. First, as Lydia, the engineer working in San Jose, points out, many college-educated, professional Mexican Americans have themselves benefited from programs intended to improve minority representation in higher education and in the workplace. Volunteering as a mentor and devoting time to non-profit organizations that benefit the Latino working-class community function, in part, as a way of recognizing one's social origins. For many, such as Lydia, it is also a way to give back to the kinds of organizations and programs that helped them get where they are now.

A second explanation is suggested by Keith, the university outreach program administrator who asserted that his volunteer work was *not* motivated by a desire to benefit the Latino community, specifically. That his volunteer work does, nonetheless, benefit this group tells us something about the social context within which the respondents live. In much of the Southwest and California, Latinos now constitute over a third of the

local population. The majority of this group consists of first-generation immigrants and their children who, when compared to the rest of the United
States, are relatively young, have low levels of formal education, and experience high rates of poverty. Simply put, the ethnic concentration of Latinos in places such as San Jose and Phoenix creates a context in which
third-plus-generation Mexican Americans who are interested in volunteer
efforts that benefit disadvantaged members of the community will have
ample opportunity to do so within the disproportionately disadvantaged
Latino community. Keith's remarks notwithstanding, many third-plus-
generation Mexican Americans are likely to give significance to the connection between their own ethnicity and the origins of the communities
they volunteer in.

The third likely source of the sense of obligation expressed among the
respondents is the "Chicano ethos" identified by Garcia, that is, the lasting
sense of ethnic consciousness that first emerged among activists during
the Chicano Movement in the late 1960s. He and other social theorists
have argued that the lasting effect of the nationalist identity movements of
the 1960s and 1970s was, ultimately, not separatism, but a positive transformation of the meaning of racial and ethnic identities from a source of
shame to a source of pride. Many of the people I spoke with said their first
encounter with this form of ethnic consciousness took place during college, while they were taking a course in Chicano Studies or participating
in an ethnic identity student organization.

Ethnicity in the Workplace

Another area that has seen a significant transformation in the meaning of
ethnic identity is the professional workplace, where the Mexican Americans I spoke with were usually a clear minority. Of the fifty people I spoke
with, forty-two worked in Anglo-majority workplaces. In three of the cases,
the interviewee was the only Mexican-origin person at work. Of the
eight that worked in environments where the majority of coworkers were of
Mexican origin, four—a counselor for convicted felons, an elementary
school teacher, a community organizer, and the director of a university
outreach program for minority high school students—served primarily
the Latino community. The other four—the president of a business con-
sulting firm co-owned by his father, two managers in the same Hispanic
marketing firm, and a billing clerk—served primarily Anglo clientele.

For most of the people with whom I spoke, though they might be able to come up with a few names of Mexican Americans who had done well in their places of employment, on the whole they saw much room for improvement in terms of Mexican-origin representation, especially higher up in the organizational hierarchy. Michael spoke about how some of these issues relate to his own company: "We have a woman who's Mexican American who runs our Dallas regional office. And then we have a woman who's in charge of the office we report to in Pasadena. I believe she's half Mexican American. But there's a concern that there's still not enough when you start looking at the numbers, there's still not enough representation there."

For those working in more technology-based areas, such as engineering, Mexican-origin representation was nearly nonexistent. When I asked Sylvia, an environmental engineer living in Berkeley, what percentage of her coworkers were Mexican American, her response was: "Zero. There's nobody. There are not a lot of Hispanic engineers."

Ethnic Comfort

If, in fact, the majority of Mexican American professionals work in Anglo-majority jobs, an important question in relation to structural assimilation is, to what degree do they feel integrated in the work environment? In this regard, an interview question concerning the degree of comfort people felt around co-ethnics versus Anglos often elicited responses centering on the workplace. For a few of the people I spoke with, working in an Anglo-majority environment was not an issue. Felipe, a thirty-year-old fireman, made the following observation when I asked him if the ethnic background of his coworkers made a difference to him: "I would say no. But I've been pretty lucky in that I've never really had a problem with people. I could walk into a room with people I don't know and by the time I leave I'm shaking hands and people are telling me to call them next week, you know, let's go someplace."

Many of the Mexican American professionals interviewed, however, were quite clear about their higher levels of comfort around Mexican-origin coworkers. Margaret, an administrative assistant with a high school education at a Catholic church in east San Jose, talked about her experience in this regard at previous jobs:

> I've worked for several different companies where the majority was white, and I always got that feeling that they looked at you at a kind of lower level. So, it was kind of like you were happy to see other people

who were also Mexican who you could fall back on. You know, you'd go to meetings and say things, and [people would] look at you and say, 'that's a good point, but . . . ,' and then go on to something else. And so it was just nice to know someone and be like, God, I'm glad I'm not the only one here.

For others, the lack of ethnic representation at work is less a matter of social comfort than a recognition of a form of social inequality. Ken, for example, the financial analyst cited earlier, believes that his sense of comfort in social interactions is less important than his politically informed awareness that it is simply not good that his present workplace is lacking in ethnic and racial diversity:

I guess whenever I go into a room around here, all I see are white people. I immediately know, you know, there are only white people here. Not that I become uncomfortable with white people, because I know them and they're good people. I get uncomfortable because I look around and it's like there's not a lot of color in here. I notice that sort of thing whenever I go places and I try to surround myself with more than that. So, it's not being uncomfortable with the people, it's just being uncomfortable with what I'm recognizing.

An earlier generation of Mexican Americans might have been content in knowing that someone like Ken had the opportunity to arrive at his position. The people I spoke with, however, were more likely to be concerned about equality of outcomes, that is, proportionate representation at the workplace.

Ethnic Identity and Corporate Culture

Though most of the interviewees expressed a sense of dissatisfaction with the low representation of ethnic coworkers, some felt that, in the face of corporate culture, little could be done to improve the likelihood of interaction with co-ethnics at the workplace. Cara, a job recruiter for a major product manufacturer in the San Francisco Bay area and also an active member of a Hispanic professional organization, argues that, despite some degree of racial and ethnic diversity at her place of work, corporate culture tends to isolate her as a minority professional from others of her background.

Cara: The friends that I do have at work, they're all white, for two reasons. One, the people that I'm meeting in my job—I'm meeting with managers, I'm meeting with directors, and most of those people are white. And then, most of the people who are Hispanic, or the women who are Hispanic, are like the admin, or secretaries, or, you know, the cafeteria. . . . It's just corporate culture, you know. I mean, I don't know if you've ever worked in a company before, but like, all the managers eat together, and the middle managers eat together, and, you know, the people who are like on your level kind of stick together and, you know, it's just that they happen to be white.

Cara's comments suggest that even in workplaces where other Hispanics are present, differences in social class and unspoken expectations regarding with whom one may associate work to impede co-ethnic interaction. That is, though the ideal of the Chicano ethos holds that you identify with and relate to your working-class roots, corporate culture, reinforced through the social segregation of workers by education and occupational status, often prevents this from occurring in practice at the workplace.

For Bernard, a twenty-something financial analyst working for a multinational bank in San Francisco, the pressure to conform to corporate culture extends far beyond the office.

Bernard: At the workplace, I definitely don't fit in. For example, what do people at work do on the weekends? They go to Tahoe, they go golfing, they talk about certain things, boating or whatever. Or, their tastes in music are different. Their tastes in many things are different. A lot of times I feel as though I can't have extended conversations with people at work because I'm speaking a different language than they are. I don't know anything about golf. I have never been yachting.

TM: Do you ever feel you need to learn more about these things in order to fit in?

Bernard: Oh, definitely. For example, at work I definitely feel that for me to get ahead and succeed in business and in my job it's essential for me to assimilate, somewhat, or at least become knowledgeable of certain subjects. For example, just golf, or going to Tahoe, at least knowing what I'm talking about. Because, the reality is, that's what people do in my business, and if I want to fit in and not be seen as an outsider, I need to learn about it, or I need to start golfing, which my friends and I have discussed. We want to start golfing, just because, strictly business-wise, it will help us.

A few of the Mexican American professionals interviewed were frank about their efforts to take up golf, learn about fine wines, and regularly read the *Wall Street Journal* as ways of conforming to some of the expectations of corporate culture. Both Cara's and Bernard's remarks reflect an awareness of the class dynamics that, in the professional world, appear to force the choice between maintaining allegiance to your ethnic/racial group and assimilating to Anglo-dominated corporate culture. However, as many of the interviewees suggested in their responses, identity politics has made the distinction between professional identity and ethnic identity much less clear. Cara, who is also an active member of the Hispanic Business Society, provides a good example. Though, as she argues above, corporate culture often prevents her from establishing relationships with co-ethnics at work, she feels she can take advantage of the diversity outside of work in the San Francisco Bay area and her membership in ethnic organizations to maintain her ethnic ties.

> Cara: I think partly because my job doesn't provide any camaraderie or professional interaction with other people of color, I have to look for that outside of my job, which I do, with different organizations. I seek it out because you have to. You have to actively seek it out. I think I'm lucky because I'm in the Bay area, because I can't imagine being in an area where there aren't very many Hispanics. You know, so what if you're more comfortable with Hispanics, there isn't anybody else.

One response to the low percentage of minorities in the workplace among Mexican American professionals, which follows plainly from the assumptions of structural assimilation, is simply to try to fit in. Another response, however, which represents a more recent innovation in efforts at social integration, was to join ethnic identity professional associations. In organizations such as the National Society of Hispanic MBAs (NSHMBA) and the Society for Hispanic Professional Engineers (SHPE), the Mexican American professionals I spoke with found the kind of ethnic camaraderie and moral support they do not often have access to at their place of work. It should be noted that many of those involved in ethnic identity professional associations were also active in non-ethnic professional associations, including engineering societies, chambers of commerce, and other profession-specific organizations, such as the California Bar Association.

Thus, third-plus-generation Mexican Americans professionals are not joining ethnic identity associations because they are being excluded from non-ethnic ones. That is, ethnic identity professional associations are not serving as "parallel institutions," in Gordon's sense of the term. Instead, the people I spoke with often supplement their experience in the over-whelmingly Anglo-majority professional world through the contact they have with *co-ethnics working in the same or similar field in ethnic identity professional organizations.*

I stress this last point because I believe it represents a marked depar-ture from the ethnic voluntary associations prominent at mid-century. It would appear that ethnic organizations at the beginning of the twenty-first century have become, to a large degree, professionally specialized. This represents a development worthy of further investigation. That a Mexican American professional would be more likely to join, say, the Association of Latinos in Public Financing and Accounting than the local chapter of LULAC might imply that ethnicity has become yet another method through which to expand one's list of potential business contacts.

On the other hand, mentoring and scholarship programs, as well as professional development workshops sponsored by these organizations, have been designed to improve minority group representation in specific professional areas. This raises the possibility that these new forms of ethnic organization have become more efficient and targeted than earlier forms in promoting the integration of outside groups into mainstream in-stitutions. Other research, for example, suggests that ethnic professional organizations provide this integrating function for the Japanese American community.[12] With respect to Mexican Americans and other Latino groups, this remains, as of yet, an unexplored area of sociological research.

Both Gordon's formulation of structural assimilation and the more re-cent selective acculturation arguments made by segmented assimilation theorists give special emphasis to the formation of parallel institutions within ethnic communities as a key element in the survival strategies of ethnic groups prior to their integration into mainstream American society. Among the third-plus-generation Mexican Americans interviewed for this study, however, the lines between their professional and ethnic identities have been, to some degree, blurred. Their participation in ethnic identity professional organizations and the post-movimiento Chicano ethos now provide the social and symbolic space for the non-contradictory conflu-ence of ethnic consciousness and integration with mainstream America.

Ethnic Work

In contrast to those who believed their place of employment marginalizes their ethnicity, five of the respondents believed that their ethnicity directly influences the kind of work they do. In four of these cases, all of which concerned jobs related to Latino marketing, this was primarily a matter of choice. Gloria is an account manager at a Phoenix firm that specializes in Hispanic advertising. When I asked her if being Mexican American had affected her choice of work, this is what she said: "It has motivated me to want to work more heavily with the Hispanic community whether it be through my job or volunteering. It's something that's very important to me. I mean, I know I grew up here and maybe I was more assimilated, but I think we can all find a common voice, and I think that it's something I'm going to be working with for quite a while." As is the case with volunteering, the mere size of the population in the Southwest assures that people like Gloria, who would like to do work somehow connected to the Latino consumer market, will likely find an opportunity to do so.

Vicki, a high school math instructor from Mesa, Arizona, provides an interesting contrast to those who deliberately chose a "Hispanic" or "Latino" position. Though she enjoyed her work with Latino students, during our discussion about English as a Second Language (ESL) courses she revealed that her placement in classes with predominantly Spanish-speaking students was not her choice and had nothing to do with her actual language skills.

TM: So, have you taught ESL classes, then?

Vicki: No, not ESL classes, per se, but since my last name is Herrera, they used to put all of the Mexican kids into my classes. Thinking that I spoke Spanish, they would automatically do that. So, I would have a classroom full, and I would be the only one who didn't know Spanish.

TM: Was that ever an issue?

Vicki: You know, I worked with it because the only negative thing was I wished that I could communicate better. But as the year progressed, that was less of an issue. I liked those kids because they would always be really hardworking, extremely hardworking. And, many times, their knowledge of math was beyond what we were doing, and I would try to get them into the higher-level classes.

TM: And so you never felt that you might have gotten the short end of the stick because you had to work with non-English speakers and others didn't?

Vicki: Well, only a couple of times, like when they gave me the lowest math level class with fifty students. You know, beyond that, no, and when it was a regular size class, I felt okay with it. I mean, I really did kind of struggle, but I wouldn't say short end of the stick. I would look at it and say, you know what, they are my ethnicity, it's my responsibility to help so, no, I don't feel like I got the short end of stick. I knew it was a bigger challenge.

Ethnic work appears to be a distinctive feature of the current structure of structural assimilation. Certain positions in the workforce are designated ethnic jobs, preferably occupied by ethnics. By being disproportionately assigned Spanish-speaking students to her class, despite the fact she did not speak Spanish, Vicki provides a striking, and problematic, example of this. That Vicki, in fact, enjoyed working with first-generation Latino children, does not justify the fact that this was an ethnic assignment not of her own choosing. This contrasts with the experience of the four other respondents doing ethnic work in the area of "Hispanic marketing," who chose from the beginning to work in those ethnically designated positions.

Of course, both public education and marketing are professional areas that have had to adapt and are still in the process of adapting to the rapidly growing U.S. Latino population. It may be that Latino demographic growth provides an area of synergistic opportunity for college-educated Mexican Americans who wish to work in occupations that address the needs of this burgeoning group. On the other hand, if ethnic work implies that otherwise-talented Mexican American professionals are being channeled into more difficult work with a disadvantaged population, or that they are serving a clientele with considerably less financial resources than other market niches, such assignments may instead represent a systematic lowering of economic and work opportunity for some individuals on the basis of ethnicity. Such a pattern has, in fact, already been observed among black professionals who disproportionately cater to an African American market.[13] Thus, for a variety of factors, including the segregation of work assignments, equality of outcomes for race and ethnic groups at the workplace is still all too often an unattained ideal. One strategy that has attempted to address this situation over the years with mixed results is a set of federal laws known collectively as Affirmative Action.

Mexican Ethnicity and Affirmative Action Policy

Perhaps no change in the landscape of structural assimilation is more striking than federally mandated Affirmative Action policies. These laws have been implemented either through executive order or Supreme Court ruling since the early 1970s and are designed to increase the presence of underrepresented minorities and women in certain sectors of the workforce and higher education. While the majority of the people I spoke with were in favor of Affirmative Action, most were quick to point out their belief in merit. Though Affirmative Action could facilitate acceptance into a competitive college or career track, ultimately, it was up to the individual to prove his or her academic or professional ability.[14] As Keith, the university outreach program director, puts it,

> I strongly, strongly believe in a meritocracy. But one of the shortcomings of a meritocracy is that it assumes equal opportunity. And in the United States they preach meritocracy, but they practice inequality. For example, Proposition 209 in the state of California tied the hands of state agencies in their ability to look at gender or ethnicity as a factor in determining either contracts or admissions. And I believe in that, if you have a meritocracy. And then, only if you have a meritocracy that is fed by a school system that is based on equal resources. But the reality is we don't have equal resources. We have schools that are heavily, heavily deprived, that have a large number of children coming from poor backgrounds, a large number of limited English proficiency students, and they have a demand and need for resources that another school in Los Gatos [a wealthy suburb northwest of San Jose] doesn't have to worry about.

Beyond the unequal opportunity identified by Keith, other respondents, such as Rosemarie, a Silicon Valley researcher in her late thirties, believe that persistent stereotypes of Mexican American students also justify maintaining some form of Affirmative Action policy. As she argues, "Mexican students, regardless of how well they're performing, are the target of a negative stereotype that they're lazy, they don't study, their parents don't care about education. So, that's why I think Affirmative Action has to be there to help ameliorate those differences." Rosemarie went on to describe how, despite taking all honors courses in junior high, she was initially tracked in an unchallenging curriculum at her Anglo-majority high school. It was only through the intervention of her parents, both college-educated, that she was returned to a curriculum that matched her abilities.

As the above examples demonstrate, the respondents' justification of their support for Affirmative Action policy rested on (a) their observation that there are very few minorities in the mainly white-collar settings where they work; (b) the unequal access to resources, especially quality education, experienced by the Latino population; and (c) persistent stereotyping and racism on the part of mainstream society. The underlying sentiment expressed by the people I interviewed was that meritocracy would be ideal. Lamentably, it was also clear that the premise of equal access to resources upon which meritocracy is based has yet to be attained. Until this occurs, programs like Affirmative Action will be necessary to assure minority representation in higher education and the workplace.

Coworkers' Doubts and Reverse Discrimination

Despite the generally favorable position taken on Affirmative Action, a few respondents, such as Claudia, a planning director for a Phoenix non-profit organization, expressed a sense of ambivalence towards this federal policy designed to improve minority representation:

> I struggle with it because I see the need for it. How are some folks who are qualified going to get in? There are still going to be some barriers for them. But I don't like the way other folks view it, making you feel as if you weren't qualified, that you only got where you are because of Affirmative Action. I don't like that. So, it would be nice if we could get rid of it and judge people just on their qualification, but I just don't see that happening.

For Felipe, a Phoenix firefighter in his early thirties, comments by Anglo coworkers suggesting that he benefited from "reverse discrimination"—that is, qualified whites were passed over so he could be selected for the position—led to a personal crisis of confidence that he, with the help of his girlfriend, was eventually able to resolve. I asked him about this during our discussion about Affirmative Action.

> TM: Has it ever come up as an issue at work that you may have benefited from Affirmative Action?

> Felipe: Yeah, when I was working as a reserve, I decided to test for Phoenix, and after a couple of tries I eventually got the job. And I found out that somebody there where I used to work said the reason I got the job was because they needed to make an ethnic balance. And you know, I thought about it, and was thinking, well, who the hell would say that? Then I started thinking, well, I wonder if that's true? And I told my girlfriend, and she asked me point blank, how many times did you test

before you got hired? And I go, twice. And the very first time that you tested, were you ready for the test? And I go, no, not completely. I was ready for the physical part of it, but I just missed passing the written exam. And then she asked me, the second time that you tested, were you ready? And I said, hell yeah. And, she goes, did you pass? And, I go, hell yeah. Did you do okay, good, or great? I kicked ass, I said. And she's like, well, then don't pay attention to them. They're only saying that because they know it's going to bother you. So, yeah, I had that thrown in my face one time. And, it was…, it was really disturbing.

As is evident in Claudia and Felipe's remarks, some respondents experienced a degree of ambivalence towards policies that were occasionally the source of self-doubt, especially when used by white colleagues to undermine minority accomplishments and explain their own failures. Affirmative Action thus represents a kind of double-edged sword in the manner in which it has transformed the way outside groups are integrated into the major institutions of American society. In the past, groups deemed by mainstream society to be unfit for entry into certain occupations and institutions of higher education were either unambiguously uninvited or turned away at the door. Today, federal law now compels employers and universities to recognize and include these formerly excluded groups.

But as many of the interviewees attest, the formal inclusion of underrepresented groups does not preclude their ongoing informal exclusion. In fact, the results of redistributive social policy that targets underrepresented groups are rather easily reinterpreted by members of untargeted groups as evidence that minority colleagues are lacking in individual merit. This is apparently the price, often paid at the psychological level by minority professionals, of a set of federal laws that have done much to improve the presence of underrepresented groups in areas from which they have been historically excluded.

Ethnic Professional Identities

Over the last forty years, higher levels of ethnic consciousness and government programs targeting minorities have worked to create a context in which race and ethnicity are matters of public concern. In direct contrast to the experience of ethnic groups during the first half of the twentieth century, members of minority groups who have attained some degree of socioeconomic advancement are integrated into a context in which race and ethnicity are, at least ostensibly, matters of public concern. Whereas, before it could be assumed that integration into mainstream institutions of middle-class employment meant checking your outsider status at the door, today, minority employees are allowed and motivated to maintain their racial and ethnic affiliations.

As Garcia argues, the Chicano ethos has evolved, such that a growing ethnic consciousness and social integration with mainstream America are no longer contradictory tendencies. To the contrary, as comments of the respondents attest, increased integration into higher education and the professional workforce may actually increase ethnic consciousness, especially in relation to an increased awareness of the low levels of minority representation in these "host" institutions. This last point should make clear the distinction between the ethnic or racial consciousness of minority groups and the "symbolic ethnicity" of the descendants of European immigrants—minority identity is still closely tied to persistent racial and ethnic inequality.

In spite of underrepresentation at the workplace, a connection between ethnicity and occupation was maintained through the many ethnic identity professional associations the respondents chose to participate in. Though the sample for this study disproportionately selected Mexican Americans involved in these types of organizations, the aforementioned decline in more broad-based Mexican American organizations that are not profession-specific suggests that, at the very least, a change in the basis of volunteer organization for this group has occurred. The extent to which ethnic associations are now organized on the basis of professional specialization is a matter of further empirical investigation.

In sum, the interview data suggest that the structure of structural assimilation has changed as the activist politics of the 1960s and 1970s have led to the creation of federal policies that recognize the need to improve minority representation in the workplace. At the same time, the politics of ethnic pride and empowerment have raised individual-level group consciousness among historically aggrieved minorities, such as Mexican Americans who, in the post-1965 era, are unlikely to see their professional and ethnic identities as mutually exclusive. That this consciousness is slightly soured by accusations of "reverse discrimination" on the part of some Anglo colleagues did not appear to neutralize the interviewees' generalized perception that inequality of opportunity and representation on the basis of ethnicity is still a fact of everyday life.

Having dealt in this chapter with elements of the political structure that have shaped Mexican American ethnicity, in the next chapter we will consider more demographic issues. Ongoing immigration from Mexico, the size of the Mexican-origin population within a city, and differences in socioeconomic status between groups, as we shall see, also have an impact on how people think about themselves, who they get to know, and even with whom they are likely to become intimately attached.

4 The Social Contours of American Mestizaje

Typically in a book of this nature you would expect to come across early on, perhaps in the second chapter, a broad profile of the ethnic or racial group being studied, delineating its socioeconomic status and relative standing with respect to other groups in society. Or, in a book of a slightly different nature, you might expect to find primarily qualitative work based on ethnographic research or personal interviews with little reference to population data. An underlying theme in this second type of book is likely to be a critique of the use of quantitative methods that privilege top-down categories over individual assertions of self-identity and actual human experience. I admit to falling somewhere between these two camps, refusing to accept aggregate numbers as the necessary starting point of investigation, while also not dismissing large-scale identities as merely convenient mechanisms for the management of large-scale populations.

The socially constructed nature of mestizaje requires that we look at both its experiential and aggregate qualities. Reasons for looking at the experiential level should already be apparent. In chapter 2 we read how third-plus-generation Mexican Americans are able, using the cultural resources available to them and their relationships with co-ethnics, to patch together an American-born ethnic culture likely to persevere long past the second generation. And in chapter 3 we learned how ethnicity structures the day-to-day lives and opportunities of this group in organizations and at the workplace. Having touched on the matter of social structure, however, now would be a good time to step back a bit to consider some of the key demographic elements that provide the context for and constrain the social integration of third-plus-generation Mexican Americans today.

To begin with, it is apparent that the viability of mestizaje as a meaningful social construct depends on the existence of official categories potentially threatened by racial and ethnic intermixing. This was true in seventeenth-century New Spain, and it is still true today, I believe, in the United States, though in the case of colonial-era Latin America a stronger argument can be made for the existence of a purely top-down assignment of racial topologies. In contrast, since the late 1960s, group-specific advocacy organizations in the United States, such as the NAACP, the National Council on La Raza, and the Japanese American Citizens League, have played influential roles in helping to determine the official categories of race and ethnicity found on government forms such as the U.S. census.[1] Though clearly politically derived, these categories are not arbitrary and are, in fact, necessary to measure systematic forms of ongoing minority group discrimination and inequality. Moreover, they ensure the enforcement of anti-discrimination legislation, such as the Civil Rights Act of 1964, the Voting Rights Act of 1965, and the Fair Housing Act of 1968.[2] It may, in fact, be the case that census categories such as Hispanic/Latino/Spanish and even Mexican American/Chicano/Mexicano are, to a large degree, political constructions, but to the extent that they allow us to gauge the unequal treatment of the groups they define, they have real social meaning and are thus empirically useful.

Despite their usefulness, there is evidence that these official categories are blurring and beginning to overlap one another. Fortunately, social researchers using quantitative data do not simply accept the existing categories. Instead, additional information, such as education, occupation, household income, and intermarriage, is often used to get at ambiguity and internal ethnic group diversity. Demographers Barry Edmonston and Jeffrey Passel, for example, project the size of the Latino population in the year 2050 to be anywhere from 16 percent to 29 percent of the total population, assuming average levels of annual immigration.[3] This wide range of possibility thus reflects not the uncertain volume of future immigrants arriving from Latin America, but rather the uncertain nature of self-identity among the members of this group, the boundaries of which are not clearly drawn. Analyses of 1990 census data show that approximately 30 percent of Latinos have an Anglo spouse or partner, and that of the 5.4 million children in the United States who have at least one Latino parent, approximately a quarter of them live in households with one Anglo parent.[4]

Intermarriage among Latinos appears to be increasingly correlated with an important component of social class. Qian (1997) found that approximately 60 percent of married Latino males, ages twenty to twenty-nine with a college degree, had a non-Latino spouse in 1990 (as compared to 53 percent in 1980). The rate for Latina women with the same characteristics is even higher, at 66 percent (48 percent in 1980).[5] An accurate assessment of the status of the Latino and Mexican American population,

Table 4.1 Estimated size of Latino population by generation and ethnicity*

Ethnicity	1st	2nd	3rd+	Total
Mexican American	10,163,734	7,997,942	6,913,176	25,073,952
	(40.5)	(31.9)	(27.6)	(100.0)
Puerto Rican	1,343,903	1,136,980	741,002	3,221,885
	(41.7)	(35.3)	(23.0)	(100.0)
Cuban American	927,610	329,867	119,018	1,376,495
	(67.4)	(24.0)	(8.6)	(100.0)
Other Latino	4,367,987	2,056,205	1,341,296	7,765,488
	(56.2)	(26.5)	(17.3)	(100.0)
All Latinos	16,803,234	11,520,094	9,114,492	37,437,820
	(44.9)	(30.8)	(24.3)	(100.0)

Source: Current Population Survey, March 2002.
*Generation percentages for each ethnicity in parentheses.

then, must take into account the fact that many of its members, and especially the better-educated among them, are marrying non-Latinos and will raise children whose ethnic identity is far from certain.

For all the insight they offer, recent sociological studies of Latino intermarriage have been weak in their ability to disaggregate the population beyond its foreign-born and native-born components.[6] This is largely due to their reliance on census data, which do not consistently provide information regarding the respondent's parents' country of origin. The fact that the Mexican-origin population in the United States contains both the largest segment of current immigration, as well as a sizeable adult population with roots extending well beyond the second generation, makes this group a good match for a multiple-generation data set. As can be seen in table 4.1, the U.S. Mexican-origin population constitutes approximately two-thirds of the entire Latino population and has within it the largest third-plus-generation component (27.6 percent). In fact, the size of the third-plus-generation Mexican American population alone is larger than the entirety of any one of the national-origin-specific Latino subgroups.

In this chapter, I use national data from the 1994–2002 Current Population Survey (CPS) to assess the social integration of the Mexican-origin population in the United States over three generations. The focus is on one of the principal measures used by sociologists to measure the social distance between two groups: cross-group intermarriage. Before heading in that direction, however, I would like to provide a brief overview of the demographic profile I mentioned above, which one might expect to see in a study such as this. My hope is that, by the end of the chapter and the discussion of intermarriage, you will have a better sense for the permeability of the aggregate categories so precisely referred to below.

Three Generations of Mexican Americans: A Comparative Look at Socioeconomic Status

Table 4.2 is based on estimates from the 2002 Current Population Survey and compares the Mexican American population to the entire population of the United States. The first generation is defined here as individuals not born in the United States, the second generation as those who were born in the United States but have at least one foreign-born parent, and the third-plus 'generation as U.S.–born individuals whose parents were also both born in the United States. Already, however, we can see how categorical fuzziness may creep in and complicate our analysis. For example, some social scientists have suggested using the "1.5 generation" as a separate category to define immigrants who arrived in the United States as children.[7] Presumably, their experiences of cultural adaptation and socialization are quite distinct from those who arrived as adults. Also, one might consider any number of possible combinations for what I define here as second-generation Mexican American, including those with, say, one fourth-generation parent or those with a non-Mexican-origin parent. Nevertheless, for the sake of parsimony and, admittedly, because of the limitations of the data with regard to the respondent's age at immigration and parents' ethnicity, in this chapter I will adhere to the standard array of first-, second-, and third-plus-generation categories defined above.

Set beside the U.S. population as a whole, of which more than three-fourths are third-plus generation, the Mexican American population is more evenly distributed among the three generations, the first generation being the largest. With a 41 percent concentration of people between the ages of zero and nineteen, the age distribution of Mexican Americans approximates an inverse of the U.S. population as a whole, where 43 percent of the population is over the age of forty. What table 4.2 does not tell us is the varying contributions by generation to the Mexican American age categories. For example, 67 percent of the second generation is under the age of twenty and makes up over half (51 percent) of all Mexican Americans

Table 4.2 Selected characteristics of Mexican Americans compared to the entire United States population

	Percentages	
Characteristic	Mexican Americans	All Americans
Generation		
First	40.5	12.8
Second	31.9	10.7
Third-plus	27.6	76.5
Age		
0–19	40.7	28.6
20–40	36.7	28.3
Over 40	22.5	43.2
Region		
Texas	27.1	7.5
Southwest	9.6	4.1
California	40.0	12.2
West	5.0	6.5
Midwest	8.7	22.6
South	7.2	28.2
Northeast	2.4	18.9
Total	25,073,952	282,081,975

Source: Current Population Survey, March 2002.

in that age category. In contrast, largely because of the time in life when people are most likely to migrate, only 17 percent of the first generation is younger than twenty, while 52 percent is concentrated in the twenty to forty age range. The third-plus generation is somewhat more evenly distributed by age, though there is still a high concentration (46 percent) in the under-twenty category.[8]

The region categories in table 4.2 are as follows: California; Texas; Southwest (Arizona, Colorado, and New Mexico); West (Mountain and Pacific states, minus the Southwest and California, and including Alaska and Hawaii); Midwest (Standard Census definition); South (Standard Census definition, minus Texas); and Northeast (Standard Census definition). As expected, the largest concentration of Mexican Americans (77 percent) is still in Texas, the Southwest, and California, or what is sometimes referred to among Chicano scholars as Aztlan, the mythical homeland of the Aztecs and the actual homeland of the majority of Mexican Americans living in the United States today. That said, evidence from the 2000 census suggests the fastest *rates* of growth of the Mexican-origin population have taken place outside Aztlan, in regions such as the South and Midwest.[9] These changes in the geographical distribution of the Mexican-origin population present intriguing opportunities for social scientists interested in exploring the effects of different regional contexts on the social integration of this group, a matter which we will return to shortly when looking at intermarriage.

Tables 4.3 through 4.5 give us a comparative sense for levels of social inequality among three generations of Mexican Americans, and among third-plus-generation non-Hispanic whites and blacks. The general cross-generational trend for Mexican Americans is that, though there are impressive socioeconomic gains made between the first and second generation, the gains between the second and third generation are less impressive and often negligible. Consider first educational attainment. In table 4.3 we see that rates of high school graduation approximately double between the first and second generation. Though the difference between the second and third-plus generation is notable, about a quarter of all adult Mexican Americans whose families have been in the United States for more than two generations do not have a high school diploma, a figure lagging far behind that of third-plus-generation whites, and four percentage points behind third-plus-generation blacks. On the other end of the scale, the second- to third-plus-generation change in college graduation rates is incremental, with only 10 percent of third-plus-generation Mexican Americans completing a bachelor's degree, the lowest figure of the three groups presented here.

Turning to table 4.4, we see similar cross-generational changes with regard to occupational status. The percentage of Mexican Americans working in management positions ("executive, administrative and managerial"), areas of professional specialization, and administrative support positions triples from the first to second generation, while the percentage working in agriculture ("farming, forestry and fishing") drops by three quarters. Again, however, the changes from the second to third-plus generation are marginal at best. Though the 20 percent of employed third-plus-generation Mexican Americans working in higher-status managerial

Table 4.3 Educational attainment percentages by generation and ethnicity in the United States (age 20 and older)

Education level	Mexican-origin generations			3rd+ generation	
	1st	2nd	3rd+	Whites	Blacks
<High school diploma	63.9	27.2	24.9	10.7	20.7
High school diploma	21.8	34.9	36.4	33.1	34.9
Some college	9.5	29.8	28.7	28.7	29.7
Bachelor's degree	4.8	8.2	10.0	27.5	14.7
Sample size	6,314	1,781	2,896	88,483	14,496

Source: Current Population Survey, March 2002.
Note: Weighted proportionately with Current Population Survey population weights.

Table 4.4 Occupational status percentages by generation and ethnicity in the United States (age 20 and over)

Non-military occupations*	Mexican-origin generations			Third+ generations	
	1st	2nd	3rd+	Whites	Blacks
Executive, administrative, managerial	3.5	10.8	11.6	17.5	9.8
Professional specialty	2.3	9.1	8.4	17.6	11.9
Technicians, related support	0.6	3.3	4.0	3.4	2.9
Sales	5.6	11.1	9.7	12.1	8.7
Administrative support, including clerical	5.6	20.2	19.1	13.7	16.7
Service	23.9	14.7	15.8	10.6	21.7
Precision production, craft, repair	18.2	13.8	13.9	11.3	7.2
Machine operators, assemblers, inspectors	12.4	5.1	5.3	4.4	7.4
Transportation, material moving	5.4	4.7	5.3	4.2	6.5
Handlers, equipment cleaners, helpers, laborers	11.4	4.6	5.0	3.0	5.9
Farming, forestry, fishing	11.1	2.7	1.9	2.2	1.2
Sample size	4,566	1,254	2,109	65,070	9,414

Source: Current Population Survey, March 2002.
*Less than 0.1 percent of each group in the sample held military positions.

Table 4.5 Family household income percentages by generation and ethnicity in the United States

Income	Mexican-origin generations			Third+ generation	
	1st	2nd	3rd+	Whites	Blacks
<$20,000	26.0	19.9	17.9	10.1	28.3
$20,000–39,999	35.5	27.3	26.3	20.8	27.4
$40,000–59,999	18.6	22.8	22.2	20.2	18.5
$60,000–79,999	9.4	13.8	15.9	16.7	12.1
$80,000+	10.5	16.2	17.6	32.1	13.6
Sample size	2,728	768	1,236	37,223	6,119

Source: Current Population Survey, March 2002.

and professional specialty positions is just about equal to the percentage of these categories for third-plus-generation blacks, it lags considerably behind that of third-plus-generation whites, who have over a third of their employed adult population working in these areas.

Household income (table 4.5), as well, shows only incremental improvement between the second and third-plus generations. The percentage of low-income households among third-plus-generation Mexican Americans is still relatively high, if a bit lower than that of third-plus-generation blacks, over a quarter of whose households have an income of less than $20,000. This last point is all the more remarkable since blacks, on average, have higher levels of educational attainment than Mexican Americans. Though racial inequality and discrimination in the job market may have a role in explaining this incongruity, another contributing factor is differences in family structure. On average, the Mexican-origin family household is less likely to be headed by a female than that of blacks and also more likely to have "non-nuclear" family members contribute to total household income.[10]

In sum, a cross-generational comparative look at Mexican American progress in education, occupations, and income provides limited support for the classical assimilation approach to social integration, through which the socioeconomic status of U.S. ethnic groups sees solid gains with the emergence of each new generation. Instead, adult Mexican Americans show striking improvements in education and occupations between the first and second generation, but then appear to congeal at the third generation and beyond into an overwhelmingly working-class population, a tenth of which has attained a bachelor's degree and a quarter of which has not graduated from high school. As will be demonstrated shortly, these relatively low levels of educational attainment have a direct impact on the broader question of social integration among Mexican Americans across generations.

Mexican American Intermarriage

Sociologists give two primary justifications for engaging in the study of intermarriage. First, it is an excellent way of measuring social distance among different groups in society. For example, the fact that endogamy, or in-marrying, among blacks between the ages of twenty to twenty-nine is about 95 percent, while that of like-aged Asian Americans is about 36 percent, tells us something important about the social distance between each of these two groups and the rest of U.S. society.[11] Namely, marriage data broadly suggest that Asian Americans are much more likely to have intimate relationships with people outside of their racial group than are African Americans.

Second, given its role as an important mechanism through which distinct race and ethnic groups become socially entangled, some theorists argue that high rates of intermarriage serve as a primary indicator of assimilation and social integration into mainstream society.[12] This last observation is consistent with Gordon's (1964) argument that intermarriage occurs well along the arc of assimilation, preceded by "acculturation" and "structural assimilation."[13]

In the present context of ongoing Mexican immigration, however, I argue that assimilation-based theories of social integration focusing on cultural and social characteristics of individuals do not adequately account for the varying contexts within which the Mexican-origin population across the United States currently lives. In certain regions of south Texas, for example, over 90 percent of the population is of Mexican-origin, whereas in other parts of the country, such as the Pacific Northwest where there are also multiple generations of Mexican Americans, this figure is closer to 5 percent. Similarly, average differences in educational attainment between Mexican Americans and Anglos vary by region, as well. Such variation, which has become more apparent in recent decades as the Mexican-origin population has increased its presence in regions outside the ethnically concentrated states of California and the Southwest, provides a unique opportunity to examine the effects of social structure on social integration.

Ongoing immigration itself may have varying effects on different parts of the Mexican-origin population, and its impact on intermarriage is unclear. From a cultural pluralist perspective, ongoing immigration from Mexico may serve to reinforce Mexican identity and community, encouraging ethnic bonds across generations, slowing down the process of assimilation, and decreasing the likelihood that even native-born Mexican Americans would marry outside their group.[14] Others have argued quite the opposite. High levels of ongoing immigration may instead lead to higher levels of competition for resources within an ethnic group, such that forms of ethnic solidarity and social organization deteriorate.[15] In such a context, ongoing immigration would not be associated with lower rates of intermarriage and might even encourage it. A more complete understanding of social integration as a process thus requires that, along with individual characteristics, we look at the social context that shapes individual opportunities for inter-group interactions.

Before arriving at the specific contexts of integration for Mexican Americans, we should know exactly with whom this population tends to marry. Table 4.6, based on a pooled national sample of the 1994–2002 Current Population Survey, shows the rates of intermarriage by generation for Mexican husbands and wives between the ages of twenty and thirty to major U.S. race and ethnic subcategories. The percentages for both sexes are quite similar and show that, across generations, the vast majority of Mexican Americans tend to marry other Mexicans Americans. This finding differs from that based on the intermarriage rates of European Americans for whom, according to sociologist Richard Alba, "a long-term trend of increasing intermarriage that dates at least to the immediate post–World War II period and probably earlier, has made marriage across ethnic lines now the rule rather than the exception."[16] Still, there is an out-marrying trend such that by the third-plus generation, about 45 percent of Mexican Americans in the specified age category is married to non–Mexican Americans.

The group to which Mexican Americans are most likely to be intermarried is non-Hispanic whites, or Anglos, who make up 24.9 percent of the spouses for men and 26.5 percent of the spouses for women in the sample.[17] The second group most likely to intermarry with Mexican Americans is other Latinos (3.6 percent for both men and women), a category that does not include either Cuban Americans or Puerto Ricans, but does include people of Central and South American origin. Given the historical geographic concentration of Cuban Americans and Puerto Ricans in East

Table 4.6 Mexican-origin intermarriage percentages by race, ethnicity, and generation (ages 20–30)*

Spouse's race/ethnicity	Generations of husbands				Generations of wives			
	All	1st	2nd	3rd+	All	1st	2nd	3rd+
Mexican-origin	65.4	73.1	66.3	55.4	63.2	70.8	64.3	55.4
Puerto Rican	0.8	0.5	1.3	0.7	0.7	0.7	0.7	0.6
Cuban American	0.1	0.1	0.2	0.1	0.3	0.2	0.4	0.2
Other Latino	3.6	5.4	2.2	2.3	3.6	4.4	4.2	2.5
Non-Hispanic white	24.9	15.8	24.3	36.4	26.5	17.6	25.4	35.5
Non-Hispanic black	1.8	1.8	1.2	2.1	2.7	2.5	2.3	3.4
American Indian	0.5	0.3	0.7	0.5	0.4	0.4	0.3	0.5
Asian American	3.1	3.1	3.9	2.5	2.6	3.5	2.4	2.0
Sample size	2,744	1,168	619	957	3,456	1,183	985	1,288

Source: Current Population Survey Outgoing Rotations, 1994–2002.

*Cases are weighted proportionately by Current Population Survey population weights. To reduce the number of marriages in the sample occurring prior to immigrating, only individuals residing within the United States for at least ten years at the time of the survey are included.

Coast cities, low levels of Mexican American intermarriage with these groups is not surprising. Even by the first generation, the clear majority of intermarriages take place with Anglos, and by the third generation, Mexican American men in the sample are more likely to intermarry with Asian Americans, and Mexican American women with blacks, than they are with other Latinos. At least with respect to inter-ethnic intermarriage, there is little to suggest here that Mexican Americans are contributing to the formation of a cross-generational fusion of Latino subgroups. Instead, even beyond the second generation, Mexican Americans show a strong tendency to intermarry with people of like ethnicity. Outside of this dominant pattern, the most likely source of inter-marital fusion is through pairings with non-Hispanic whites.

Given the dominant mode of intermarriage with Anglos and the low sample numbers of intermarriage for other groups in the Current Population Survey (CPS), the remainder of the chapter will focus on Mexican American/Anglo intermarriage. In table 4.7 we see some of the stark differences in rates of Mexican American/Anglo intermarriage across regions of the United States for men and women, ages twenty to thirty.

Table 4.7 Percentages of Mexican-origin/Anglo intermarriage in the United States by region and generation (ages 20–30)

Region	Generations of Mexican-origin husbands				Generations of Mexican-origin wives			
	All	1st	2nd	3rd+	All	1st	2nd	3rd+
Texas	19.9	13.7	16.2	24.8	24.0	14.4	21.6	29.1
	(699)	(173)	(182)	(344)	(915)	(179)	(262)	(474)
Southwest	35.1	15.3	23.5	54.3	34.4	18.8	33.3	43.4
	(304)	(84)	(73)	(147)	(402)	(96)	(102)	(204)
California	23.2	13.6	27.2	42.5	23.2	15.5	23.3	37.7
	(792)	(440)	(173)	(179)	(961)	(450)	(301)	(210)
Other regions	47.3	31.1	54.8	70.2	51.3	35.9	52.1	70.8
	(678)	(340)	(129)	(209)	(826)	(322)	(214)	(290)
United States	27.6	17.8	26.9	39.6	29.6	20.0	28.4	39.1
total	(2,473)	(1,037)	(557)	(879)	(3,104)	(1,047)	(879)	(1,178)

Source: Pooled by author from the Current Population Survey Outgoing Rotations, 1994–2002.
Note: Sample sizes for individual cells are in parentheses. Cases are weighted proportionately by Current Population Survey population weights. Only individuals residing within the United States for at least ten years at the time of the survey are included.

Among all Mexican Americans, the regions with the lowest levels of intermarriage are California (23.2 percent for both men and women) and Texas (19.9 percent for men, 24 percent for women). In comparison, the states of the Southwest (Arizona, Colorado, and New Mexico) have combined rates of intermarriage from 10 to 15 percent higher for men and women than Texas and California. This is partly because a larger portion of the Mexican-origin population in the Southwest region is third-plus generation, but even among the first and second generations, intermarriage rates are slightly higher than those of either Texas or California.

Moving outside the area of historical concentration in the Southwest, California, and Texas, the differences in rates of intermarriage are even more striking. Outside this region, about half of all Mexican Americans in the sample are intermarried with Anglos. By the third-plus generation this figure is just over 70 percent for both sexes. (Note that the categories of

West, Midwest, South, and Northeast have now been collapsed into the single category of "Other Regions" because of the smaller sample numbers in the intermarriage data.) These "outside-Aztlan" rates of intermarriage are masked when considering aggregate national data and, among the third-plus generation, are similar to levels of intermarriage found among Italian Americans in the late 1970s, though it should be kept in mind that the vast majority of Mexican Americans still live in those states situated along the Mexican border.[18] How then, can we explain these dramatic regional differences in intermarriage between Mexican Americans and Anglos? Is there something more to this than simply regional variation in individual-level attributes and preferences for the ethnicity of a spouse? What role do contextual factors, such as the local concentration of the Mexican-origin population or average differences in educational attainment between Anglos and Mexican Americans, play in this? The next section will consider both individual- and structural-level theoretical explanations of intermarriage.

Theoretical Approaches to Intermarriage

Individual-Level Explanations

Studies emphasizing individual-level explanations of intermarriage tend to focus on factors derived directly from assimilation theory. These include a person's generation from immigration to the United States and level of education.[19] According to Gordon, generation may be understood as a measure of "cultural assimilation," or "acculturation." This assumes that the cultural patterns of individuals within a group, including language, religion, and communal organization, will tend to merge over the course of generations with those of mainstream society. Such a convergence, Gordon argues, will tend to lower the barriers of prejudice and discrimination between groups.[20]

Not surprisingly, Gordon has had his share of detractors. The critical take on acculturation tends to emphasize the ethnocentric underpinnings of its early formulations in the social sciences; its normative application in government-sponsored efforts to "Americanize" recent immigrants; and the clear disparity in power made explicit in an approach that features the acquisition by a subgroup of the cultural traits of a dominant group. Still, detached from its ideological baggage, as a way of understanding and acknowledging the changes that take place in an immigrant-origin group over time through exposure to the culture of a new country and interaction with others outside the group, the notion of cultural assimilation carries with it much explanatory power.[21]

As noted in chapter 3, Gordon proposed that "structural assimilation"— that is, entry into the mainstream institutions of work and higher education—provides a greater challenge for American ethnic groups seeking to improve their life chances than did cultural assimilation. The children of immigrants, after all, readily acquire language skills and the essentials of American popular culture. It is the difficulty of establishing relationships across class-delineated categories of ethnicity—the "ethclass"—that sets the biggest obstacle in the way of social mobility.[22]

For all the criticism brought to bear on his theory of assimilation over the last forty years, there is a certain sociological eloquence in Gordon's formulation worth emphasizing. Simply put, when it comes to social integration, the crucial differences among groups in society are not the more superficial cultural ones that tend to be transformed as fast as the younger generation is willing to adapt. Rather, the important differences are those concerning advantageous relationships that may provide access to opportunities outside the ethnic community. As any network theorist would be quick to point out, it is often the case that your most advantageous relationships are your acquaintances—the friend of a friend who you may barely know—and not your close friends or family. "Weak ties," as they are sometimes referred to, work to our advantage because they link us up with people we would not normally encounter.[23]

Your best friend, as it turns out, is often not the best source for finding out information about a new job, for example, since more often than not the two of you know the same people. Your best friend's second cousin, Marjorie, however, whom you met only briefly at a weekend barbeque, may link you up with a universe of opportunities that you otherwise would not be aware of precisely because of her social distance from your circle of friends and family. Though Gordon makes no mention of weak ties in his work, his notion of structural assimilation, which holds that people in an ethnic group are at an advantage when they develop relationships with people outside their ethnic community, is consistent with more recent developments in social theory.

Educational attainment serves as a good measure of structural assimilation. The educational system is, after all, one of the most important institutions in modern societies for providing both opportunities for socioeconomic advancement and interactions with members of other groups.[24] At the individual level, then, we should expect higher levels of acculturation and structural assimilation, measured by immigrant generation and educational attainment, respectively, to yield lower levels of social distance between Mexican Americans and Anglos, and, hence, higher levels of intermarriage. Though previous studies have found support for the application of both cultural and structural assimilation theories to explain Mexican American intermarriage, none have done so using national-level data and a separate category for the third-plus generation.[25]

Social Structural Explanations

Explanations based on social structure for intermarriage are strongly influenced by Peter Blau's classic work, *Inequality and Heterogeneity* (1977), in which he argues that inter-group relations are closely tied to the question of relative group size and stratification.[26] That is, beyond the matter of individual characteristics and preferences, the prevailing social structure strongly determines the opportunities for interaction between different groups. The expected role of relative group size in this approach may be stated succinctly, as smaller groups will have more interaction with outside groups than will larger groups. Despite cultural affinities among fellow ethnics, when ethnic groups are numerically small, their members will be motivated to establish relationships with outsiders.

At the core of Blau's theory is the notion that common social characteristics facilitate interactions between different groups, which in turn facilitate integration. From this perspective, ongoing immigration may serve as a font of cultural distinctiveness that functions at the aggregate level, through linguistic or religious differences, for example, to negatively impact inter-group interaction and thus discourage intermarriage.[27] If lower rates of intermarriage with outside groups occur in the Mexican American population in the cities where there is a relatively high percentage of Mexican immigrants, all else being equal, we would have support for a cultural pluralist argument. That is, high rates of immigration tend to encourage ethnic group solidarity. If, on the other hand, a larger immigrant population is correlated with higher rates of Mexican Americans marrying outside their group, this would imply that ongoing immigration disrupts ethnic group cohesion, drawing attention to internal group differences of generation and culture and making it less likely that a person in a group with higher levels of immigration would marry someone of the same ethnic group.[28]

Apart from cultural differences, one may focus on socioeconomic status as the crucial social characteristic determining inter-group integration. With regard to intermarriage, "internal status diversity" and "between-group status inequality" have emerged as key explanatory factors.[29] A basic understanding of social stratification implies that if there is more socioeconomic diversity within groups than between groups, there will be higher levels of social integration among these groups and, thus, higher rates of intermarriage. Imagine, if you will, a society made up of three different ethnic groups. Each group differs from the others in terms of cultural traditions and contains within it people from a variety of education, occupation, and income backgrounds. That is, each of the three ethnic groups is culturally homogeneous, but socioeconomically diverse.

Now consider a second society that contains three different ethnic groups that also differ on the basis of cultural traditions. In contrast to the first society, however, each of these groups is socioeconomically concentrated: the first group consists of the owners of all the major businesses and corporations in society; the second group consists primarily of government workers and management; and the third group consists of wage earners in retail and factory production. According to a basic understanding of social stratification, in the first society, where there is much status diversity within each group but little status inequality between groups, we would expect high levels of social integration across groups, despite cultural differences. There would simply be ample opportunity to meet people of different ethnic group backgrounds in school, across occupations, and in neighborhoods where people of all three different backgrounds could afford to live. In the second society, in contrast, where there is little status diversity within groups, but much status inequality between groups, we would expect that socioeconomic differences between groups would work only to reinforce cultural differences and, thus, lower the likelihood of integration between groups.

With regard to intermarriage then, an ethnic group with much internal status diversity will likely have much higher rates of intermarriage with outside groups than one consisting overwhelmingly of a single class status. Moreover, we would predict that the greater the difference in average status between two groups, the lower the likelihood of interaction between the two groups and, hence, the lower the likelihood of intermarriage between them.[30]

A related issue not necessarily tied to economic stratification, but which should be controlled for nonetheless, is the sex ratio within an ethnic or racial subgroup. Deviation from a one-to-one, male-to-female ratio should increase the likelihood of intermarriage for the subgroup as a whole, since members of the sex with larger numbers will be motivated to seek partners outside the group. Furthermore, unobserved regional differences, such as historical antagonism between groups or a shared regional culture, may also impede or facilitate inter-group interaction and should be controlled for when looking at aggregate measures of social structure.

In combining both individual- and metro-level variables in the same statistical models, I follow the example of recent work that views assimilationist and structural perspectives as complementary and integrates them in a multilevel approach.[31]

Data and Findings

The data for this chapter were pooled nationally from the 1994–2002 Outgoing Rotations of the Current Population Survey (CPS). Individual cases used in the sample were restricted to those individuals living in Metropolitan Statistical Areas (MSAs) where there were sufficient cases in the CPS data to construct the city-level variables used in the analysis. In all, 137 metro areas from thirty-nine states are represented in the sample.

The CPS is ideal for this research because of its oversample of the U.S. Hispanic population and because of the questions it began including in 1994 regarding the respondent's parents' birthplace. This last feature allowed me to disaggregate the Mexican American population by first, second, and third-plus generations. The sample used for this research consists of individuals of Mexican origin who, at the time the survey was taken, were between the ages of twenty and thirty. All individuals who selected "Mexican American," "Mexican/Mexicano," or "Chicano" as their "Spanish ethnicity" in the survey are defined here as being of Mexican origin. The age restriction serves to minimize any confounding effect that divorce or second marriages may have on an individual's spousal choice. Presumably, married people between the ages of twenty and thirty are less likely to be remarried than older married people. In addition to being married to either a Mexican-origin spouse or a non-Hispanic white, each person in the sample had been in the United States for at least ten years. This last criterion helps assure that the marriage took place within the United States and also serves to select individuals who are more likely to have a long-term commitment to staying in the country.

After the respondents were selected based on the above criteria, they were linked by household with their spouse to create two separate records, one for women and one for men. No age restrictions were placed on spouses. Low numbers in the CPS data of intermarriages between Mexican Americans and other minorities, including non-Mexican-origin Latinos, made comparisons of intermarriage to other groups impractical. For a more detailed overview of the data, methods, and variable definitions used in this chapter, please refer to Appendix IV.

Descriptive Statistics

Frequency and percent intermarried data for categorical variables are provided on the top portion of table 4.8. On the bottom portion of the same table are listed mean and standard deviation data for continuous variables. Beginning with gender-specified rates of intermarriage, we see that, in agreement with earlier studies, Mexican American wives in the sample are slightly more likely to be intermarried with Anglos than Mexican American husbands. As in the Mexican-origin population in general, a large portion of the sample has not completed high school (39.1 percent of men, 31.2 percent of women) and relatively few have completed college (5.8 percent of men, 7.1 percent of women). The effects of structural assimilation, however, are suggested through the correlation of higher percentages of intermarriage with higher levels of education. A similar relationship between the three categories of generation and percent intermarried suggests a trend of cultural assimilation.

Among the region categories, California and Texas, respectively, have the largest concentration of the Mexican-origin population, constituting together over three-quarters of the sample. In fact, the Los Angeles metro area alone makes up 17 percent of the sample. Though there are signs that the Mexican-origin population is growing rapidly in other parts of the country, it is still a population that is overwhelmingly concentrated in the states just north of the Mexican border. Across regions, there are noticeable differences in the gender disparity of intermarriage, with the greatest differences occurring in Texas and in the Other Regions category. In both of these categories Mexican-origin wives are 5.7 percent more likely to be married to an Anglo man than are Mexican-origin husbands to an Anglo woman.

Looking at the continuous variables, we see that the average Mexican American in the sample lives in a metro area where just a little under 32 percent of the local population is also of Mexican origin. The standard deviation around this average ranges from 10 to 53 percent. So, although

Table 4.8 Percentages or means in the Mexican-origin population for selected variables (ages 20–30)

Variables	Husbands		Wives	
	Percent of sample	Percent intermarried	Percent of sample	Percent intermarried
Entire sample	100.0	25.7	100.0	28.3
Categorical variables				
Education				
<High school diploma	39.1	17.8	31.2	17.3
High school diploma	34.6	27.4	35.8	27.8
Some college	20.6	32.4	25.9	36.9
Bachelor's degree	5.8	45.2	7.1	48.6
Generation				
First	44.3	16.7	35.4	19.5
Second	23.0	23.9	29.9	27.6
Third-plus	32.6	39.1	34.7	37.9
Region				
Texas	31.1	18.1	32.8	23.8
Southwest	7.6	36.8	8.0	36.2
California	45.0	23.1	43.8	23.3
Other regions	16.3	42.2	15.4	47.9
Continuous variables	Mean	Standard deviation	Mean	Standard deviation
Percent Mexican-origin	31.2	22.1	31.7	22.0
Percent foreign-born	38.1	11.0	37.6	11.3
Status inequality	1.66	0.16	1.66	0.17
Status diversity	4.59	0.37	4.59	0.37
Sex ratio	1.10	0.20	1.09	0.20
Sample size	1,996		2,485	

Source: Author's calculations based on data from the Current Population Survey Outgoing Rotations, 1994–2002.

the average Mexican American lives in a city where about a third of the population is also of Mexican origin, there is considerable variation with regard to the experience of Mexican ethnic concentration across the United States. The percent of foreign-born in the local population is closer to 38 percent for the average person in the sample, with the standard deviation for this figure about half that for percent Mexican-origin.

Status inequality between Mexican Americans and Anglos is calculated by simply dividing the Anglo educational attainment average in a given MSA by the Mexican-origin average in the same metro area. Status parity between Anglos and Mexican Americans would be reflected in a value of 1.0 for this variable. Any number greater than 1.0 would indicate status inequality in the favor of Anglos, who on average tend to have higher levels of educational attainment than Mexican Americans. The mean rate of status inequality among MSAs in the data set is 1.66, which is significantly higher than the level of parity. Though there were a few metro areas in the sample that approached a 1.0 level of inequality—notably St. Louis, Missouri, and Little Rock, Arkansas—the vast majority of people in the sample lived in cities where Mexican American/Anglo inequality in educational attainment was considerably higher.

Logistic Regression Analysis

In this section we will consider the determinants of Mexican American intermarriage using a statistical technique known as binomial logistic regression. This approach is quite useful when considering an issue that has only two possible outcomes—that is, zero or one, yes or no, male or female. In this case, I want to understand what determines whether a Mexican American marries (a) another Mexican American, or (b) an Anglo. A helpful feature of logistic regression is the "log-likelihood" coefficients it produces. With a simple mathematical transformation (e^x, where x equals the log-likelihood coefficient), logistic regression coefficients can be interpreted as odds-ratios. Odds-ratios are convenient since they serve as a relatively intuitive way of understanding probability, not unlike when rolling dice (five-to-one odds for a given side on a given roll) or thinking about the lottery (million-to-one odds of hitting the jackpot, for example). The two logistic regression models presented in table 4.9 thus predict the log-likelihood that a person of Mexican ancestry will marry an Anglo as opposed to another Mexican American, given a set of explanatory variables.

Model 1 includes the two individual-level assimilation variables, educa-

Table 4.9 Estimated coefficients of selected logistic regression models of Mexican American intermarriage with Anglos

Variables	Model 1 Husbands	Model 1 Wives	Model 2 Husbands	Model 2 Wives
Education				
<High school diploma†				
High school diploma	0.314*	0.476***	0.335*	0.506***
Some college	0.520***	0.916***	0.577***	1.005***
Bachelor's degree	1.047***	1.365***	0.989***	1.467**
Generation				
First†				
Second	0.512***	0.315*	0.597***	0.311*
Third-plus	1.268***	0.899***	1.242***	0.886***
Region				
Texas†				
Southwest	1.002***	0.654***	0.369	−0.086
California	0.694***	0.229*	0.364*	−0.376*
Other regions	1.668***	1.387***	0.324	−0.026
Structural variables				
Mexican-origin concentration			−0.031***	−0.033***
Percent foreign-born			0.000	0.024**
Anglo/Mexican-origin status inequality			−2.066***	−1.910***
Mexican-origin status diversity			−0.652***	−0.311
Sex ratio			0.384	−1.026**
Intercept	−2.671***	−2.311***	4.597**	3.976**
N	1,996	2,485	1,996	2,485
-2 log–likelihood	2,044.7	2,700.9	1,934.9	2,577.2
Chi-square	229.4***	261.5***	339.2***	385.2***
df	8	8	13	13

Source: Author's calculations based on data from the Current Population Survey Outgoing Rotations, 1994–2002.

†Reference category, *P < .05, **P < .01, ***P < .001 (two-tailed tests)

tion and generation, with region as a control variable. As hypothesized above, structural assimilation, measured by educational attainment, and cultural assimilation, measured by immigrant generation, are statistically significant and associated with a higher likelihood of intermarriage for both men and women. The effect of education, however, is a bit stronger for women than that of generation, while the reverse is true for men. A wife with a bachelor's degree is nearly four times more likely to be intermarried ($e^{1.365}$ = 3.918) than is a wife without a high school diploma. In contrast, a husband with a bachelor's degree is only 2.8 times more likely to be intermarried than one without a high school diploma ($e^{1.047}$ = 2.849). Intermarriage for Mexican American husbands is instead more strongly influenced by the effects of acculturation, measured here by immigrant generation. Relatively acculturated third-plus-generation Mexican American husbands are 3.5 times ($e^{1.268}$ = 3.553) more likely than their first-generation co-ethnics to be intermarried. The same comparison among wives yields a multiple of only 2.5 ($e^{0.899}$ = 2.457).

The regional categories in Model 1 are also statistically significant and show that Mexican Americans living outside Texas have a greater likelihood of intermarriage than those living in Texas. Consistent with the finding in table 4.2, the category with the strongest positive effect on Mexican American/Anglo intermarriage is that of other regions. That is, Mexican Americans living outside the areas of highest Mexican ethnic concentration (the Southwest and California) have the highest likelihood of being intermarried with Anglos.

The set of metro-level structural variables are introduced in Model 2. The addition of these variables effectively nullifies the effects of the regional categories seen in Model 1, with the exception of the statistically significant effect of California for both men and women. Overall, regional differences in the likelihood of intermarriage appear to be largely attributable to differences in varying elements of social structure across MSAs. In particular, the Mexican-origin concentration within MSAs has a strong and statistically significant negative effect on intermarriage for both sexes. This provides additional support for previous research pointing to the centrality of group size as an explanatory factor in understanding the intermarriage of Mexican American and Anglo populations within a city.[32] The relationship between Mexican ethnic concentration and the probability of intermarriage with Anglos is virtually identical for husbands and wives. This is demonstrated graphically for third-plus-generation Mexican Americans with a high school diploma in panel A of figure 4.1.[33] There we see

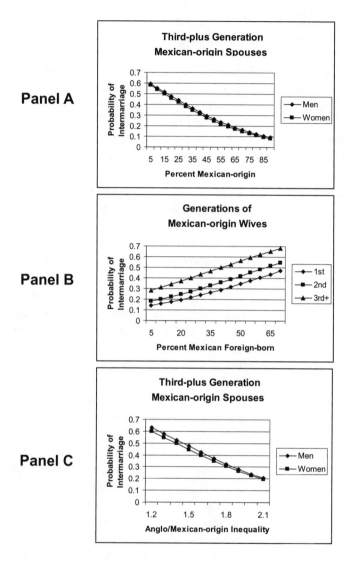

Figure 4.1 Predicted probabilities of Mexican American/Anglo intermarriage by selected independent variables. *Panel A.* Third-plus-generation Mexican-origin spouses and ethnic concentration. *Panel B.* Generations of Mexican-origin wives and percent foreign-born. *Panel C.* Third-plus-generation Mexican-origin spouses and Anglo/Mexican-origin inequality. (*Source:* Author's calculations based on data from the Current Population Survey Outgoing Rotations, 1994–2002)

in a near straight-line fashion that the higher the percentage of Mexican Americans in a local population, the lower the probability of intermarriage with an Anglo spouse.

The measure of ongoing immigration, percent foreign-born in the local population, produced an unexpected gender-specific result. The coefficient of this variable for husbands is zero and not statistically significant. For wives, the percent foreign-born variable is statistically significant and positive. There thus appears to be no supporting evidence in the data for either spouse that ongoing immigration itself reinforces ethnic solidarity across generations. If that were the case, we would expect a lower probability of intermarriage with Anglos for people living in cities with higher rates of Mexican immigration. For Mexican-origin wives, however, it appears that higher levels of Mexican immigration are associated instead with a higher probability of intermarriage with an Anglo. The reason for this, however, is unclear. One possibility is that among Mexican-origin women in the marriage market, there is a hierarchy of preferences for potential Mexican American husbands in which first-generation males are at the bottom. As the percentage foreign-born increases in the Mexican-origin marriage pool, Mexican-origin women may be motivated to pursue partners outside their ethnic group. This explanation seems particularly plausible in light of (a) the fact that men's success in the marriage market in general depends more strongly than women's on their economic circumstance; and (b) the low levels of educational and occupational attainment found among first-generation Mexican immigrants.[34]

That this effect is statistically significant in a model that controls for inequality within the Mexican-origin population, however, suggests that the perception among Mexican-origin women that first-generation males have low economic potential may be at least as important in the marriage market as their actual economic potential.[35] This effect for Mexican American women is shown graphically in panel B of figure 4.1. There we see that, across generations, as the percentage of Mexican immigrants in the population increases, the probability of intermarriage with Anglos increases.

In a fashion very similar to the effect of Mexican-origin concentration, Anglo/Mexican–origin inequality—measured here by the ratio of differences in educational attainment between the two groups within each MSA—also has a negative, statistically significant effect on intermarriage. The pattern is apparent for both sexes, though it appears to be slightly stronger for men than women, as is evident in panel C of figure 4.1. This is consistent with Blau's and others' research, which points to the centrality of socioeconomic stratification in understanding the integration of subgroups in a society. Specifically, the greater the inequality between two groups, the lower the level of integration between them—a fact reflected here in the lower probability of intermarriage between the two groups in question.

Mexican-origin status diversity, in contrast, did not produce the expected result. Instead, higher levels of ethnic group status diversity based on educational attainment were associated with a lower probability of intermarriage for both sexes, though this variable was statistically significant for men only.[36] A possible explanation for this unexpected result is that higher levels of status diversity among Mexican Americans may be more a reflection of higher representation in the local ethnic population of those with low levels of educational achievement (e.g., a grade school education or less) rather than of those with high levels (a bachelor's or graduate degree). If that is indeed the case, then it would not be surprising that "diversity" would lower the probability of intermarriage.

The last variable in Model 2 of table 4.9 is the sex ratio, which operated as expected. A higher ratio of Mexican-origin men to women is associated with a higher likelihood of intermarriage for husbands and a lower likelihood for women, though this effect is statistically significant for women only.

Discussion

In this chapter, the probability of Mexican American/Anglo intermarriage is shown to be highly correlated with both individual-level and contextual factors. At the individual level, Gordon's primary forms of assimilation, "cultural" and "structural," prove to be strong determinants of intermarriage with non-Hispanic whites for the Mexican-origin population. Both the amount of time one's family has been in the United States, measured here by generation, and the degree of participation in mainstream institutions, measured here by education, are positively correlated with a higher likelihood of intermarriage with the majority population. The addition of the third-plus category to the generation variable highlights an important gender difference in the intermarriage patterns of Mexican Americans with Anglos. Namely, the probability of intermarriage for wives is more strongly influenced by their education than it is for men, for whom intermarriage is more strongly determined by acculturation. Beyond this distinction, the overall effect of individual-level factors suggests that the process of social integration for Mexican Americans is quite similar to that of other groups who over the course of generations have blended into American society. This, however, is by no means the end of the story.

The ongoing expansion of the Mexican-origin population beyond the American Southwest and the entrance of many of its members into the middle class provide for greater variation with which to investigate the effects of ethnic concentration and stratification on the integration of this group into American society. With this additional information we see that patterns of intermarriage are not the same for Mexicans Americans in different parts of the country. Intermarriage between Mexican Americans and Anglos is higher in those areas with lower concentrations of the Mexican-origin population and where there are lower levels of social inequality between the two groups.

The role that ongoing immigration from Mexico plays in shaping the social context within which intermarriage takes place is central to this analysis. In the short term, controlling for other factors, the size of the Mexican immigrant population appears to have a direct effect on the Mexican-origin marriage market by positively affecting the likelihood of intermarriage for Mexican American wives across generations while having no effect on Mexican American husbands. As discussed above, this gender-specific effect likely results from a hierarchy of spousal preferences among Mexican-origin women, in which Mexican immigrant men occupy a low rank.

In the long term, ongoing Mexican immigration, driven largely by the economic disparity between the United States and Mexico and the dependence of the United States on low-wage labor in the agricultural, industrial, and service sectors of the economy, cumulatively shapes social context through its impact on ethnic concentration and social inequality.[37] The long-term social impact of ongoing immigration is especially evident in the border states of the Southwest, where multiple generations of Mexican Americans reside together in the same cities and often in the same neighborhoods. This situation differs markedly from the experience of either European Americans or blacks, neither of whom have been impacted to the degree Mexican Americans have over recent decades through the perpetual renewal of the first generation. Largely as a result of ongoing immigration, the average Mexican American now lives in cities where nearly a third of the local population shares their ethnicity. Moreover, most Mexican Americans live in regions where the disparity in educational attainment between themselves and Anglos are considerable, an important factor when trying to understand the nature of social distance between these two groups.[38]

As the findings in this chapter demonstrate, in the abstract and controlling for the appropriate contextual variables, the Mexican American pattern of intermarriage over generations appears quite similar to that of European Americans. Holding constant factors such as ethnic concentration and inequality, individual-level variables such as acculturation and educational attainment serve as key predictors of the probability of intermarriage for Mexican American men and women, much as they have for Italian Americans, Jewish Americans, and Polish Americans during their generations lived in the United States.

In the real world, however, in the context of high ethnic concentration and severe inequality with Anglos, Mexican American marriage patterns in the regions they are most likely to live—that is, in the states that line the U.S.–Mexico border—appear much more like that of a multiple-generation permanent minority. At the same time, the varying effect of on-going Mexican immigration on Mexican American/Anglo intermarriage in different regions of the country implies that minority status for Mexican Americans within the United States is more contextually based than that of blacks. Hence, a contextual model of assimilation is needed that directly addresses the special relevance of ongoing immigration for the multiple-generation Mexican American population. Such a model will advance our understanding of this rapidly growing component of U.S. society more effectively than one derived primarily from the experience of other racial and ethnic groups with their own distinctive histories.

In the case of the relatively well-educated third-plus-generation people interviewed for this book, we have seen that the level of ethnic concentration in cities like Phoenix and San Jose perpetuates a rich symbolic and relational landscape for those who live there. Such a context goes far in reinforcing a positive sense of Mexican ethnicity through both the consumption of ethnic culture and participation in the ethnic community. As will be shown in the following chapter, there is a flip side to the collective benefits of Mexican ethnic concentration and the social inequality that usually accompanies it. From the outside, the view of the Mexican-origin population in these settings can be, at best, slightly distorted and, at worst, prejudiced against even those whose families have been in the United States for generations. That is, the context of integration across generations appears to be shaped as much by the identities and cohesion of those inside the Mexican American community as by the perception of the community from the outside looking in.

5 Mexican-Origin Identities Past the Second Generation

Roberto is a native of East San Jose in his early forties who has worked for most of his adult life in community service, often in programs administered by the Roman Catholic Church. A few years before we met for his interview, he worked at a Catholic parochial school in Detroit as a liaison for the growing population of Latino immigrant families in that community. As he describes the scene, one Friday afternoon he was in the basement of the school cleaning out a large room. He was preparing it for use as both an office and meeting place for an after-school youth program he was putting together. Dressed casually in shorts and a baseball hat, he was moving boxes when the following incident took place.

> Roberto: So, this nun walks in, looks at me, and doesn't say anything. She's just gesturing and she points at the trash can and she's gesturing at me to pick it up. She's doing this for a couple of seconds and I go, you know, I speak English. And she goes, oh, great, it's about time they hired a janitor that speaks English. And I say, you think I'm a janitor? And she says, you're standing by the trash. And I say, I'm cleaning my office. I'm the community liaison here that you guys desperately need. Do you treat everybody who's not white like this? And she turned red and says, No, don't think that I'm racist. And I say, well you were! 'Cause this made me really mad. So, I talked to the superintendent on Monday, and he made her apologize.

Roberto, who self-identifies as Chicano, has a very clear sense of what this identity means to him, especially with regard to his participation in the local community through the Catholic Church. Yet, his Mexican ethnicity was not simply a matter of what he asserted it to be. Instead, Roberto found the assertion of his Mexican ethnicity to be at odds with the expectation of that ethnicity by others, in this case, a Roman Catholic nun.

This account and others related to me by the people I interviewed suggest that Mexican ethnicity within the United States today is far from attaining the "symbolic" or "optional" status described in the sociological research on European Americans. Over the last twenty years or so, these studies have tended to stress the "thinness" of third- and fourth-generation European-origin identities. Richard Alba's work in this area, for example, provides evidence for the "twilight" of Italian American ethnicity. By this, he means that, through a variety of measures, including intermarriage, educational attainment, political attitudes, and income, third- and fourth-generation Italian Americans are nearly indistinguishable from the rest of American society.[1] Aside from their identity as Italian Americans, he is hard pressed to find distinctive traits that mark this group as separate from the mainstream. In her study of third- and fourth-generation descendants of European immigrants, Mary Waters found that ethnic identity is not a determining aspect of these individuals' lives and instead has a more voluntary quality to it.[2] Ethnicity for this group, most of whom have various ethnic origins to choose from, is selectively utilized as a way to "spice up" an otherwise bland suburban lifestyle by preparing certain ethnic dishes, or perhaps celebrating a uniquely ethnic holiday such as St. Patrick's Day or Columbus Day.

A few of the third-plus-generation Mexican Americans I spoke with also had a voluntary quality to their ethnicity. The ability to turn on and off their ethnic identity as the social situation demanded, for example, was especially likely among those of mixed ethnic background. However, one of the more striking aspects of Mexican ethnicity among most of the people I interviewed was the degree to which it felt constrained by the expectations of non–Mexican Americans. Or, put another way, most of the people I spoke with for this study, such as Roberto cited above, could point to at least one instance in their lives where there appeared to be a troublesome mismatch between the respondent's sense of what it meant to be Mexican American and what a non–Mexican American thought it meant to be Mexican American.

The observation that Mexican ethnicity holds a relatively different status in U.S. society than European ethnicity may not strike anyone as particularly remarkable. What is remarkable, however, is that, though the sociologists mentioned above and others acknowledge that the experience of ethnicity past the second generation is likely different for people of non-European ancestry, this distinction is too often left unexplored. More often than not, it is merely assumed as the obvious contrast with which to high-

light symbolic ethnicity among European Americans. The actual meaning of ethnic identity among the multiple-generation descendants of non-
European immigrants is thus abandoned as a less interesting question.[3]

In this chapter, after a brief overview of the sociological work on ethnic identity, I directly question the application of the symbolic ethnicity
paradigm to the experience of third-plus-generation Mexican Americans.
The findings in this chapter tend to support the earlier assumption that
symbolic or optional ethnicity is a cultural privilege granted primarily to
European Americans. However, the interview data collected for this study
permit a more nuanced understanding of how non–European American
ethnic identity is constrained at the level of social interaction.

Ethnic Identity and Assimilation

One of the major adjustments made in the study of ethnicity over the past
twenty years is to acknowledge that while acculturation, structural assimilation, and intermarriage have taken place for European Americans, these
processes have not necessarily been accompanied by identity assimilation. Instead of a process through which ethnic identity gradually fades
over generations, assimilation is now marked by changes in the quality of
ethnic identity. That is, while first-generation immigrants' opportunities
and identity were strongly determined by their status as immigrants, their
third-plus-generation descendants are considerably less bound by their
ethnic affiliations. At the same time, it has been argued that ethnic identity
has become such a central part of the American experience that, contrary
to earlier assumptions, to be ethnic in the present-day United States is
to be American.[4] Put another way, a cultivated awareness of one's ethnic
origins is actually a good indication of one's assimilation into American
society.

Segmented Assimilation and Ethnic Identity

It has also been argued, however, that such a voluntary approach to American ethnicity is not equally tenable for all, most notably native-born minorities. For these groups, race or ethnicity are not options and are associated
with their social position in a permanent underclass. Their identities are
strongly constrained and determined more by the perceptions and expectations of the majority than their subjective sense of group membership.
The notion of "segmented assimilation" has been proposed as a way of

accounting for the different ways immigrant groups and their descendants are presently integrated into U.S. society.[5] Changes in the structure of the domestic economy over the last thirty years have resulted in the disappearance of relatively stable factory jobs in industry and the growth of low-wage service positions. These, combined with changes in the origins and volume of immigration since 1965 revisions to federal immigration law, have contributed to the creation of a split opportunity structure of integration. Rapid economic mobility is available for those who arrive with high levels of education and a transferable skill set. Meanwhile, people arriving with low levels of education and few transferable work skills may find their social status congealing into one of membership in a permanent underclass.[6]

A major critique of the work on segmented assimilation has been that it is still too early to tell what effect both changes in the economic structure and differences in the skill levels and education of contemporary immigrants will have on the process of assimilation. Asian and Latino immigrants who began to predominate among the flow of immigration in the late 1960s are only now beginning to witness the emergence of their third generation descendants. Assessing the applicability of assimilation theory based on the experience of the first or second generation misses the point if we consider that, even for the European groups, the process of assimilation has taken at least three or four generations.[7]

Ongoing Immigration and Mexican Ethnicity

Beyond the question of how current immigrants and their children are being incorporated into American life is the impact that current immigration is having on the experience of ethnicity among generations long established in the United States. If, in fact, large numbers of current immigrants and their children are being channeled into a permanent underclass, what impact is this having on the third-plus-generation descendants of the same ethnic group? Stanley Lieberson suggests one possibility in his classic account of race and ethnic relations in the United States, *A Piece of the Pie.* There he argues that high levels of immigration tend to create a heightened awareness of race and ethnicity among members of the dominant group, who perceive newcomers as reinforcing ethnic stereotypes. These, in turn, come back to negatively affect all members of the group, new and old, in the form of prejudice and discrimination.[8]

With regard to third-plus-generation Mexican Americans specifically,

Mary Waters, a student of Lieberson, argues that they "may enjoy some of the same intermittent and voluntary aspects of ethnic identity as Italian Americans, but the existence of a strong first-generation ethnic community, as well as of continued discrimination in housing and employment against Hispanics, would probably impose constraints on such upwardly mobile third-generation Mexican Americans that it would not on Italian Americans."[9] Significantly, in the study this passage is quoted from, *Ethnic Options,* third-generation Mexican Americans are not part of the research sample.

Research into optional identities and segmented assimilation thus both suggest an area ripe for further exploration. If, in fact, some identities are more voluntary than others, this should be evident in the day-to-day interactions ethnic group members have with others. Whereas some identities will go unchallenged as acceptable American ethnicities, others may meet with resistance from mainstream society for not meeting expectations assigned to that group. That is, it may very well be that, since the identity movements of the 1960s and 1970s, to be ethnic is to be American. But it may also be the case that some groups are understood as being more American than others. This variation in acceptance should be apparent in the degree to which an individual's ethnic identity goes unchallenged by others. The historical process through which this acceptance is determined is referred to in sociology as "social construction."

The Social Construction of Racial and Ethnic Identities

In the sociological literature on race and ethnicity, there exist many variations on the theme of how identity is socially constructed. On one end of the scale are theories that deal primarily with racial minorities and that place a heavy emphasis on the macro determinants of group identity. Omi and Winant's conceptualization of racial formation takes for granted that "society is suffused with racial projects, large and small, to which we all are subjected."[10] Some of these racial projects are racist; that is, they create or reproduce structures of domination based on essentialist categories of race.[11] An obvious example of this was the system of Jim Crow laws in the South established after the abolition of slavery. Federal and local legislation justified the legal segregation of blacks from whites on the basis of racist ideology while simultaneously reinforcing the ideology by guaranteeing the existence of a racially determined second-class citizenry.

Other racial projects, in contrast, challenge the status quo by contesting the social meaning of race. The Civil Rights Movement in the United States did just that in the 1960s when what started as a church-based movement for racial equality before the law culminated in the passage of the Civil Rights Act of 1964, the Voting Rights Act of 1965, and the Fair Housing Act of 1968. Thus, according to Omi and Winant, the "racial order" can, given the appropriate historical circumstances, be effectively challenged through the collective actions of identity-based social movements.[12] Little importance, however, is given in their approach to individual assertions of self-identity.[13]

At the other end of the spectrum are works such as Waters 1990, which focus on micro-level accounts of how European Americans are able to turn on and off different aspects of ethnic identity as the situation demands. In this approach, identity is not so much part of the social structure as it is an option. A distinction is usually made here between those whose identity is primarily voluntary and those—that is, racial minorities—who, because of their history of domination, experience their identity as being primarily determined by others.[14]

Various attempts have been made to bring together the contrasting themes of social constructionism.[15] Cornell and Hartmann have done so concisely in a graph that has on its horizontal axis a range from "assigned" to "asserted," that is, from an identity that is primarily ascribed by outside groups to that which is primarily claimed or asserted by members of an ethnic or racial group.[16] This captures nicely the outside constraints placed on individual identity while not underestimating the creative capacity of groups and individuals to produce their own identities and challenge those imposed from the outside. As Cornell and Hartmann observe, "Ethnicity and race are not simply labels forced upon people; they are also identities that people accept, resist, choose, specify, invent, redefine, reject, actively defend, and so forth. They involve an active 'we' as well as a 'they.'"[17]

For the purposes of this chapter and to make its connection to other work in social constructionism explicit, I extend Cornell and Hartmann's schema so that an identity that is primarily asserted—that is, a personal or group expression relatively unconstrained by the expectations of outside groups—would be indicative of the sort of voluntary ethnicity described in the literature on ethnic options. An assigned identity, on the other hand, would be more indicative of the structurally based racial minority status described by Omi and Winant and also addressed in the literature on segmented assimilation.

It is unlikely that a given individual will have an exclusively asserted or exclusively assigned identity. Instead, we should expect that each person's identity will consist of a combination of both asserted and assigned elements. In the remainder of this chapter, we will look at how this combination shapes the meaning and experience of identity among the third-plus-generation Mexican-origin respondents.

Asserted Identities

Responses that stressed volition and individual agency in determining Mexican-origin identity reflected the asserted aspect of ethnic identity. Though the terms Chicana/o, Mexican American, and Mexican may have preceded the respondents ethnic consciousness—they did not, after all, create these labels themselves—it is clear from their comments that they have made them their own through an active process of identity selection and the rejection of alternatives. Of the three official Mexican-origin identities offered as choices in the U.S. census, there was a notable split in the sample between those who preferred a Chicana/o identity and those who preferred a Mexican or Mexican American identity. The minority in the sample (14 out of 50) who self-identified as Chicana/o tended to be more deliberate and thoughtful about their ethnic identity, something many of them took on as their own while in college. Self-identified Mexicans and Mexican Americans, on the other hand, tended to define their ethnicity more in terms of a positive contrast to other identities they rejected, such as Chicano or Hispanic. The organization of this section reflects this split. The favoring of Mexican or Mexican American identity over Chicana/o identity found in this and other studies is discussed further at the end of the chapter.

Chicanas and Chicanos

Rick is an assignment editor for a local television newscast in Phoenix. He is in his early thirties and married to a second-generation Mexican American woman. I asked him why he identified more closely with Chicano than with Mexican-origin identities. This was his response:

> Just because, you know, the third generation, we're more American-ized than if you're Mexican American. I mean if I had to choose between Chicano and Mexican American, it would be almost equal, but I'd say more Chicano than I would Mexican American. I think they're about the same thing. Chicano is more someone like myself, you know,

living in the Southwest, being more Americanized than just Mexican American. It's just easier to identify as Chicano.

When I asked Rick if there was a time in his life when he decided he would identify as Chicano, he recalled a course on Mexican American culture he had taken at Phoenix Community College. It was there, he said, that he began getting involved in student organizations and becoming more conscious of his ethnic identity. Other self-identified Chicanos in the sample also pointed to college as an important period in life when the opportunity to meet other people with similar backgrounds, often through participation in an ethnic identity organization, solidified, if not brought about, their primary identification as Chicanos. Ironically, as we shall see in the following section, those who preferred Mexican or Mexican American as their main ethnic identity tended to associate the term Chicano with people who were less educated or had a lower social status.

Rick's observation that to be Chicano is to be, in a sense, more Americanized was shared by other Chicanos in the sample. This is consistent with findings at the national level that Chicana/o identity coincides with more generations spent in the United States, with first-generation immigrants being the least likely to accept this identity as their own. It is also consistent with the claim of the ethnic revivalists, which asserts that, in the post–Civil Rights Era, to be ethnic is to be American.

Though for most self-identified Chicanas/os in the sample, becoming Chicana/o involved a kind of transformation that often happened in college, one woman interviewed experienced her Chicana identity in a more holistic manner. Eva is a single mother in her late twenties with a degree in criminal justice. She works for a contractor to the municipal court in Mesa, Arizona, that provides counseling and rehabilitation services for convicted felons.

> Eva: Well, I guess I'm real proud of who I am. And I guess in all aspects of my work and growing up and everything, I've always associated with people like me. You know, I speak my language every day at work. I try to teach my son that. So, I believe like everything I do, I do because I'm a Chicana.
>
> TM: So, was there a time in your life when this was kind of a realization?
>
> Eva: No, I think it's been like my whole life. Just growing up as a little girl, all the things I used to do, like I used to dance the *folklórico* dance.

With my parents, you know, just being a Catholic, going to church, doing all these kinds of things had everything to do with my culture.

Eva is an example of someone whose Chicana identity permeates much
of her day-to-day life. Though she lives in a predominantly Anglo suburb in
Mesa, Arizona, she shares the house with her sister and maintains strong
ties with her parents, who still live in the mining community 50 miles away
where she grew up. The birth of her son, whose father is African American, has made her particularly aware of the importance of maintaining
family ties and cultural practices, especially Spanish language, which she
is able to use at work in the court system and which she speaks to her son
regularly.

For others in the sample, however, Chicano identity appears less em-
bedded in structures of community and regular interaction with family.
David, the computer programming student, is of mixed Mexican/Anglo
ancestry. Like his father who was involved in the Chicano Movement in
Texas during the 1960s and '70s, David identifies as Chicano. He has light
skin, dark hair, and dark eyes, and he lives with his Anglo wife and three-
year-old daughter in a modest-sized condominium in Scottsdale. When
asked if there are things in his daily life that he associates with his Chicano
identity, he has this to say:

David: The way I define it is like when I'm in the company of Anglos, I feel most Mexican. And when I'm in the company of Mexicans,
I feel most Anglo. Being half and half I have the wonderful privilege
of being outcast by both societies [laughs]. You know, I took Spanish
in college, but I don't speak Spanish. It's like I feel most comfortable
with Anglicized Chicanos. But, I don't know, it goes the other way, too.
Like, I have conscious control over it as well and I know that as far as
my culture goes I'm white, my thinking. I was raised mostly with my
white mother in a white neighborhood with white people. Obviously
my wife is Anglo, as well, so I think that I can choose. Like when I'm
around Anglos, I know their culture and I know their system, and I can
work within it and make them comfortable with me there. And then
the same thing around Mexicans. Of course, the closer it gets to the
first generation, people who are over here working, the closer it gets to
people who are from Mexico, it's different.

TM: Do you have much contact with people who are first-generation
immigrants?

David: Yeah, when I was working in restaurants, of course. If you take any corporate restaurant they usually have a kitchen full of some illegal, some not Mexican immigrants.

TM: Did you ever try to practice Spanish you learned in school with them?

David: No, they mostly made fun of me if I tried to speak Spanish [laughs], which is interesting because they gave me a much harder time about it. I mean, the white folks I worked with would be able to practice Spanish with them, and they'd be nice and helpful with them and stuff. But, if I did, they would just make fun of me and give me shit. Yeah, I really had a lower status there.

David provides the clearest example of what sociologists have called situational, or optional, ethnicity. It is perhaps not coincidental that this aspect of ethnic identity appears most salient among those in the study who, like David, have mixed ancestry. His ability to turn on or off his Chicano identity is no doubt related to the fact that his mother is Anglo. Though, as is evident in the above excerpt, there are limits to this strategy. David mentions how, while working as a busboy in a restaurant, he felt uncomfortable around Mexican immigrant workers who showed him less respect than his Anglo coworkers for being Mexican but not knowing Spanish. The optional aspect of his identity thus appears to work well only when the audience in question is Anglo or native-born Mexican American. This is an important limitation grounded in the reality of ongoing Mexican immigration, a limitation the descendants of European immigrants rarely have to confront when asserting their ethnicity.

Mexicans and Mexican Americans

Compared to Chicanas/os, the self-identified Mexican Americans I spoke with tended to take a less philosophical approach to their ethnic identity, which, in many cases, was defined negatively in comparison to alternative identities such as Hispanic or Chicana/o. As Mayra, who lives in Scottsdale, Arizona, with her half-Anglo/half-Mexican American husband, notes:

I've always just said Mexican. In fact, my friends would always ask in Georgia [where she lived for a time growing up], well, what did you put, Black or White? And, I'm like, I put Other. I'm not Black or White, you know? And, now they're like, are you Hispanic? And I'm like, no, I'm Mexican. Not that I get mad, but it's like, yeah, I'm Hispanic, I suppose. Someone made that up and that includes Mexican, but if you want to just know the truth, I'm Mexican.

Hispanic may be the official option offered on government forms and job applications, but like many of the people with whom I spoke, Mayra had a strong preference for identifying specifically with her Mexican ethnicity. This is consistent with findings from survey data, which show that on the whole, Latinos are much more likely to prefer a specific national origin identity over the more broadly defined terms Hispanic or Latino.[18] Some people I interviewed, however, go a step further and make what they feel to be an important distinction between Mexican and Mexican American identities. As Dan, a Silicon Valley engineer who lives in Gilroy, California, puts it:

> I am not Mexican. And it's a big thing. Mexicans are different people than Mexican Americans. Mexican Americans, it's almost like a whole new other people. Mexican Americans do not have a whole lot in common with Mexicans. Mexican Americans are American, but they are a different kind of American. Because, I live in Gilroy, and there are a lot of Mexicans there. Mexicans are different, Mexican people are different. Besides the obvious differences of speaking, they think differently, they perceive things differently.

In his response, Dan's definition of Mexican American depends on a particular understanding of who Mexicans—that is, Mexican immigrants—are. Though he believes his ethnicity reflects membership in a distinct cultural group within the United States, it is clear that Dan also wishes to emphasize the significance of the "American" side of his Mexican American identity.

Still others in my interview sample depend on a negative characterization of Chicano identity to explain their Mexican American identity. Leo, a divorced airline attendant in his mid-thirties, grew up in a mining town about 50 miles outside Phoenix. He presently lives in Ahwatukee, an Anglo-majority suburb in the desert foothills of Phoenix's South Mountain. He has a medium skin tone and speaks with a slight Mexicano accent. When I asked him why he identifies as Mexican American, he referred back to what his father had told him about Chicano identity growing up.

Leo: See, my dad would never check Chicano. That's too much, that's slang. He'd say, "Hey man, remember you're Mexican American, not Chicano."

TM: Did you ever think of yourself as Chicano?

Leo: No, back then my dad just thought of it as disrespectful. He said, you're Mexican or Mexican American, but Chicano is disrespectful. Or, he thought it meant that you were like some kind of New Age Mexican American. Oh, you don't want no part of that.

TM: And when did this come up as an issue?

Leo: I guess that was right about when I started college, after I came here to go to school.

Leo's statements suggest that, even if they don't identify as Chicano, people of Mexican origin must come to terms with their relationship to that identity. It is an identity that has changed forever the way the Mexican-origin population in the United States thinks about itself.[19] Again, the central irony here is that, despite the fact that many college-educated people in the sample self-identified as Chicano, there was a tendency among third-plus-generation Mexican Americans who do not identify as Chicano to associate this identity with a lower social status, or as being somehow disrespectful. This is a notable deviation from changes in group identification that have taken place among, for example, African Americans, American Indians, and U.S. gays and lesbians. In all of these groups, oppositional identities originating in times of political conflict from the groups themselves—even if they were initially rejected by many group members—eventually met with popular acceptance. This has not proven to be the case for Chicano identity. As Saenz and Aguirre observe in their study on situational Mexican ethnic identity, "There are few Chicano self-conceptions but many imputed Chicano identities in the ethnic community. Chicanismo is an icon, a stylized symbol of collective identity as of yet imperfectly realized."[20]

A good explanation for the reluctance to claim Chicano identity among the Mexican-origin population has yet to be proposed. It would appear that this particular aspect of identity ties the Mexican-origin population of the United States closer to hyphenated Americans with ancestral origins in Europe than to other native-born minority groups. The examination that follows, however, of how identities are wrongly assigned to third-plus-generation Mexican Americans suggests the contrary, as well as a possible explanation for the low popularity of Chicano as a self-identification among members of this group.

Assigned Identities and Ethnic Ambiguity

In trying to understand the way third-plus-generation Mexican Americans are assigned identities by the broader society, the most significant insights come from respondents' accounts of how identities have been wrongly assigned during day-to-day interactions, usually by non–Mexican Americans. "Bad" assignments refer to both the misapplication of an ethnic label—such as "Spanish" when the respondent prefers "Chicana"—as well as a mismatch between the meaning the respondent attaches to his or her self-identity and that which the assigner attaches to it. These bring into relief the direct ways respondents felt constrained by others' expectations and assumptions about Mexican-origin identity. In this regard, there emerged from the interviews five major groupings of erroneous identity assignments upon which the following sections are based.

Assignment Error #1: You're Not Really American, Right?

The first erroneous assignment concerns the mistaken belief that the respondent is not actually from the United States. Teresa is a third-generation Mexican American in her mid-thirties, has a degree in journalism, and has spent much of her professional career outside of the Phoenix metro area. She presently holds an administrative staff position with the City of Mesa. She related to me how some people prefer to think she is not really from the United States.

> Teresa: When I was in DC, there were some people who would ask me, so, where are you from, and I would say, Arizona. And then they would say, no, really, where are you from? And I'd say, no, really, I'm from Phoenix, Arizona. So, that was always weird because I think they always expected me to say that really I was born in Mexico but then came to Arizona. And then, they were always uncomfortable after I would say I was from Arizona. It was like, well, where do we go with that? And I get angry when people ask me that. You know, if I'm from Arizona, then you should accept that I'm from Arizona. It would really piss me off.

TM: So, does it bother you when people ask you about your background?

Teresa: No. It bothers me if they take it to that next step. You know, I don't ask people, so, are you *really* from Michigan? You know? I'm very happy to tell people I'm Mexican American.

This sort of faulty assignment is particularly jolting for third-plus-generation Mexican Americans, like Teresa, who have moved out of the Southwest for opportunities in higher education or professional advancement. At precisely the moment they feel they have in some sense "made it" and have been accepted for their accomplishments by mainstream America, they are reminded of their outsider status.

Assignment Error #2: You Must Be Some Other Non-Mexican Ethnicity

A second erroneous assignment common to many of the interviewees is what I will call "You Must Be Some Other Non-Mexican Ethnicity." Most people I spoke with who at one time or another had been assigned the wrong ethnicity related a funny story in which someone began talking to them in an unfamiliar language, or how when traveling abroad they could eavesdrop on other Americans who thought they were locals. For a few, however, especially those who felt strongly about their Mexican origins, being assigned the wrong ethnicity on a regular basis can be a bit trying. Eva, who as mentioned earlier is quite proud of her Chicana identity, relates her frustration with mistaken identities: "It's funny because no one ever thinks I'm Chicana, and I get so mad. . . . But, at work, people always come up to me and ask, 'Um, are you Asian, are you this?' And oh, I just get so mad! And I'd ask some of my coworkers, do I really not look like a Mexican? And they're like, yes, you do, it's just that people don't think you do."

The majority of the third-plus-generation Mexican Americans I spoke with had at some point in their life been mistaken for another ethnicity. In fact, only one person claimed that no one ever questioned his ethnic background because it was quite obvious, he believed, that he was Mexican American. That this experience is so common among the interviewees suggests that Mexican-origin identity, by the third generation, at least, is not as obvious to others as some may think.

Assignment Error #3: You Must Be a Super Mexican

Bob, a thirty-year-old junior high school teacher in San Jose whose father is Mexican American and whose mother is of mixed Italian and Russian descent, spoke of a third erroneous assignment that, in many ways, errs in the opposite direction of "You Must Be Some Other Ethnicity," and which I will call "You Must Be a Super Mexican."

> Bob: A lot of people assume I know how to cook certain types of food or that I should behave a certain way. Like, a friend of mine, we went to a restaurant once where they were playing ranchera music, and she's like, "Oh, [Bob], do you listen to this kind of stuff?" And I'm like, "No. I was born and raised here, I don't listen to that." And then, like tomorrow we're going to a wedding where the groom is Mexican and the bride is white, and this friend of mine is like, "Oh, you should know how a Mexican wedding goes."
>
> TM: Do you ever feel like you should know these things?
>
> Bob: No, I think it's ridiculous, it's so ignorant. People are like, "You didn't speak Spanish growing up?" And I'm like, "No, did you speak German or Dutch in your house?" I mean, my family has been here for a long time. And I know there are other Mexican Americans, maybe in California, but also in New Mexico and Colorado, who have been here for generations, and I'm sure they don't all speak Spanish. I mean, I'm sure some do and some don't, but people always assume that Mexican Americans have to speak Spanish with every generation, and they don't do that with other nationalities, like Italians. No one assumes that my mom speaks Italian. They never ask her that. But, I mean with the Mexicans, they always assume that.

Though the error of expecting near-perfect cultural knowledge of all things Mexican was common enough, Bob's reaction was somewhat unique. While he was adamant that other people's ignorance lies at the root of this problem, other respondents with similar experiences often admitted to feelings of guilt for not knowing how to speak Spanish fluently or for lacking other forms of cultural knowledge. As we saw in chapter 2, the desire to make up for things unlearned in childhood led to some respondents taking Spanish courses in high school or college, spending a college semester abroad in Mexico or Spain, or, in one instance, learning to play the mariachi trumpet. Bob's case is also unique because his non-Mexican mother is third-generation Italian and Russian, two groups for whom he feels, given her experience, the expectations of cultural mastery are considerably lower.

Assignment Error #4: It's Okay That You're Mexican

Whereas the first three erroneous assignments imply mainly a degree of ignorance on the part of the assigner concerning the U.S. Mexican-origin population, the last two contain an element of overt prejudice. Jerry, a thirty-eight-year-old funding administrator in a non-profit foundation in Phoenix, provides a prime example of erroneous assignment number four, "It's Okay That You're Mexican." After he told me that people who don't know him well don't always know that he's Mexican, I asked him if people are ever surprised to find out that he is.

> Jerry: It's happened. Yeah, especially when I was younger. I was working for [a document processing company] as an intern and I had to travel to a number of different companies, and nobody would ever think I was Hispanic. It never came up. No one ever brought it up. I mean, I was Italian, I was Hawaiian, you know. But there was this one coworker—and this was probably the only time I really ever felt offended or insulted—who turned to me after I made some comment and said, "You're Mexican?" And all of the sudden you could see that he looked at me completely different. Up until that moment, everything was fine, but as soon as he knew I was Mexican you could see that he was puzzled, and his statement was, "Wow, I would have never guessed that. I would have thought you were Spanish or something." And then his comment was like, you know, don't feel bad. You know, you don't look Mexican. At a minimum, you look kind of Spanish. So, you know, don't worry.

Here, the assigner projects onto the assigned his devaluation of Mexican American identity. Clearly, if the assigner were in the assignee's shoes he would have reason to feel somehow ashamed of his lower status. By telling him he did not "look Mexican," the assigner sought to reassure Jerry that he did not match his low expectations of Mexican Americans. Stories of such unsolicited reassurances from coworkers and friends were also common among the interviewees.

Assignment Error #5: You Must Be Spanish

A related bad assignment, "You Must Be Spanish," superficially appears to be a simple variation of assignment error two, that is, the wrong ethnicity, but as will be shown, this error is also loaded with condescension. Henry, a San Jose lawyer in his mid-thirties, spoke about his determination to reject the assignment of this apparently more socially acceptable European identity.

TM: Do people ever ask you about your background?

Henry: All the time. Usually they ask me if I'm Italian or Greek or Turkish. And every once in a while they'll come up to me and ask me if I'm Hawaiian or Filipino. But my favorite, though, is if they think you're Hispanic, they'll say, oh, are you part Spanish? I say, no, I'm Mexican. I'm sure there's Spanish in there someplace, but my family is from Mexico. But I think the worst thing done to Mexicans by Californians and Texans was to make the word Mexican a derogatory term. And that's the saddest thing because a lot of people say Hispanic or Spanish simply because they don't want to say Mexican. And every other racial group at least has a slur. I mean sure there's beaner and greaser and all that, but really the cruelest thing done was to make Mexican a dirty word. And so I make a point of saying Mexican or Chicano. And if you say it first, it takes away that derogatory meaning.

The conflation of Spanish and Mexican identity is, of course, nothing new in the United States. In the state of New Mexico, a large portion of older generation Hispanos still prefer the self-identity Spanish American over others.[21] The attempt here, however, to assign Spanish identity to Jerry and Henry above, reflects an uneasiness with the term Mexican or Mexican American on the part of the assigner that is deemed unacceptable by the assignee.

Ethnic Pride and Outside Expectations

Beginning with the interviewees' asserted identities, it is clear that many third-plus-generation Mexican Americans share with the descendants of other immigrant groups certain elements of optional ethnicity. For example, almost everyone with whom I spoke expressed the sense of pride they felt in having Mexican ancestry. As Dan, the Silicon Valley engineer, put it: "I'm very, very proud of being Mexican American. In fact, I couldn't see being anything else. You know, the best skin color, everybody wants to be brown, it's the greatest. I'm prejudiced. I feel sorry for everybody else [laughs]."

As many of the university-educated interviewees revealed, much of this pride is grounded in a knowledge of Mexican American history, often acquired in a college course or through participation in a college ethnic identity organization. This association of ethnic pride with educational attainment is in line with the findings of research on the ethnic revivalism of third-plus-generation European groups.

But, for most of the interviewees, ethnic pride extends far beyond a cultivated knowledge of ethnic history and family genealogy. Living in regions with relatively high concentrations of the Mexican-origin population makes attaining a purely symbolic ethnicity nearly impossible. For many, like Eva and Leo, regular contact with their parents and siblings is a normal part of life. Also, more than half of the married people in the sample were, like Rick and Mayra, married to Mexican-origin spouses. Far from being symbolic, ethnic concentration reinforces Mexican American identity by allowing for the perpetuation of old ethnic ties and the creation of new ones. The flip side of this, as we saw with national data in chapter 4, is that higher levels of ethnic concentration also contribute to greater levels of social distance between Mexican Americans and other groups, the consequences of which will be discussed below when we turn to identity assignments.

The association in the interviewees' minds of both Mexican American and Chicana/o identities with being American is also consistent with research findings related to European-origin optional identities. If, since the identity movements of the 1960s and 1970s, to be ethnic is to be American, third-plus-generation Mexican Americans are American, par excellence. Unfortunately, not unlike Waters' finding that European-origin ethnic pride is associated with an implicit critique of other groups—that is, native minorities that have not found economic success in American life—third-plus-generation Mexican Americans' sense of being American may sometimes be negatively defined by those who are deemed to have a lower social status. Among the people interviewed for this study, a few third-plus-generation Mexican Americans explicitly made this kind of negative comparison with Chicanos and first-generation Mexican immigrants.

The different ways that third-plus-generation European-origin and Mexican-origin people are able to negatively construct their American ethnic identities has interesting implications. Whereas, as Stephen Steinberg

(2001) has argued, descendants of European immigrants have been able to mythologize their ethnic heritage, giving a special emphasis to the cultural fitness of European immigrant groups to American life, third-plus-generation descendants of Mexican immigrants are given no such privilege.[22] Quite simply, the reality of ongoing Mexican immigration places hard limits on the degree to which immigration and Mexican culture can be romanticized. In a way, this is a positive development in that many of the people I spoke with had a realistic understanding of the processes that drive immigration, and many were sympathetic to the plight of recent arrivals in the United States whose work is seen as both needed by the U.S. economy and as an immense improvement over employment opportunities in Mexico. On the other hand, some, like Dan, were adamant about drawing clear distinctions between the third-plus generation and more recent arrivals.

The special, at times contentious, relationship between native-born Mexican Americans and Mexican immigrants alluded to in the interviews has recently received a good deal of scholarly attention after years of relative neglect. In the case of the early history of the United Farm Workers Union in California, cross-generational differences related to citizenship status led to a good deal of intra-ethnic tension.[23] In other instances, such as the political organization of the Mothers of East Los Angeles during the early 1990s, key alliances have been made that breach the barriers of immigrant generation and nationality on the basis of ethnic solidarity.[24] Fortunately, many researchers in this area have come to realize that a comprehensive account of Mexican ethnicity in the United States must include an understanding of this internal Mexican immigrant/Mexican American dynamic.

The defining characteristic of optional ethnicity, the ability to choose among ethnicities or to turn one's ethnicity on or off as the social situation demands it, was—not surprisingly—most common among respondents of mixed Mexican/non-Mexican descent. But even the members of this group found limits to the voluntary nature of their ethnic identity, limits more often than not imposed by the first generation. David, for example, felt comfortable moving in the social worlds of both Anglos and native-born Mexican Americans. However, he was at a loss when it came to interacting with Mexican immigrants at work who he felt got along better with his Anglo coworkers than with him. In that context, the combination of his Chicano identity and low Spanish ability placed him on the margins—not Mexican enough to be accepted as a fellow ethnic among immigrants, yet not Anglo enough to be accepted as a casually engaged non-ethnic. Thus, though it may be argued that third-plus-generation Mexican Americans of mixed descent do have ethnic options, it would appear that, relatively speaking, they are limited, largely due to ongoing immigration.

This research also suggests, however, that the broader society has expectations about what people of Mexican origin in general are like, which may not match up with actual Mexican Americans' asserted identities. As the excerpts in this section illustrate, for many third-plus-generation Mexican Americans, simply asserting their Mexican American identity as they themselves construct it in the face of others' expectations can be an act of defiance. In this way, Mexican American identity has much more in common with structurally based minority identities in the United States than the optional ethnicities of European Americans. In the interviews I conducted, this was most obvious to people of mixed background, like Bob, who were puzzled by the expectations others had of him based on his Mexican ancestry that were not made based on his Italian ancestry.

As other respondents observed, though, ethnic expectations are often tinged with prejudice as coworkers and acquaintances are sometimes less than subtle about the negative associations they have with Mexican ethnicity. This is made clear when reassurances are offered that a Mexican American does not "seem Mexican," or when there is an obvious uneasiness about even using the term Mexican or Mexican American. In this light, proclaiming one's Mexican American identity appears less an accommodation to mainstream expectations than a defiant assertion of one's ethnic heritage in a context where many Anglos are unwilling to accept Mexican Americans as simply another among many American ethnic groups.

This could explain third-plus-generation resistance to self-identifying as Chicana/o. Leo, quoted above, summed up the feelings of many Mexican Americans towards this term when he noted, "That's too much, that's slang." For many third-plus-generation Mexican Americans, just being accepted on equal terms as Mexican Americans is challenge enough. If, in fact, Chicano is an identity that has yet to be fully realized, it is likely because Mexican American identity has yet to be entirely accepted by mainstream America.[25] Acceptable alternatives offered by mainstream culture, such as Spanish, Hispanic, or Latino, which seek to downplay the particularities of Mexican ethnicity, though sometimes selectively utilized by the people I interviewed, were more often than not rejected in favor of a Mexican-origin-specific identity.

But why should there be any resistance among the broader society to accepting Mexican Americans as Mexican Americans and not some other Europeanized, sanitized version thereof to begin with? Race, often pointed to as a central variable in U.S. social research, likely has a role, and there is considerable historical evidence that race ideology has structured the opportunities and experience of Mexican Americans in California and the Southwest. As social historian Thomas Almaguer has argued, the settlement of this region by the United States during the nineteenth century was accompanied by white supremacist policies that systematically marginalized blacks, Asian Americans, Mexican Americans, and American Indians.[26] The legacy of this period, he argues, reverberates in the contemporary West, where "racial fault lines" continue to delineate city- and state-level politics. And recent research has confirmed that, among the Mexican-origin population, phenotypic differences correlate with differences in income, education, and occupational status.[27]

However, the fact that many European groups, including Irish, Jewish, and Italian immigrants, were also racialized upon their arrival in the United States points to the contextually dependent nature of racial categories and raises some doubt about using race as the sole explanation for the perceived devaluation of Mexican-origin identity in American culture.[28] At the very least, the fact that there exists great variation in appearance among the Mexican-origin population suggests explanations besides racial discrimination must be considered, as well.

In this regard, ongoing Mexican immigration and the ethnic concentration associated with it hold great explanatory potential. As Lieberson has argued, in times of high-volume immigration, stereotypes made by the dominant society against immigrants are reinforced and often applied to the members of the group who have been in the United States for some time.[29] As discussed in chapter 4, intermarriage data also suggest a structural explanation for the social distance maintained between Anglos and the Mexican-origin population, as there are lower rates of Anglo/Mexican–origin intermarriage in regions of the United States where there are higher levels of Mexican ethnic concentration.

On the level of social interaction, then, it should not be surprising that "bad assignments" are given by the dominant group to those with whom it maintains a good deal of social distance. There is no escaping the fact that Mexican immigrants are the numerically largest and least educated of all contemporary immigrant groups. Moreover, because of the question of legal status, they have been made easy targets for political scapegoating.

Taken together, these characteristics make the acceptance of Mexican immigrants and, by association, that of their U.S.–born ethnic brothers and sisters all the more tenuous. There is also an element of class at play here that is evident in many of the interviewees' remarks. In much of the United States, but especially in regions such as California and the Southwest that have experienced high levels of ongoing immigration and where Latinos make up the bulk of the working class employed in the low-wage service sector, many Anglos simply do not associate Mexican Americans with middle-class status. Hence, it was not unusual for the people I spoke with to detect a degree of cognitive dissonance in people's expressions or comments upon learning that a Mexican American professional or college graduate was actually Mexican American.

Conclusion

This exploration of asserted and assigned identities among socially integrated third-plus-generation Mexican Americans suggests that, though this group does enjoy certain elements of voluntary ethnicity—most notably a strong sense of cultural pride and a hybrid ethnicity through which being Mexican American and Chicana/o is very closely tied with being American—societal expectations, reflected here in terms of "errors of assignment," constrain the degree to which its identity can be considered voluntary. In many cases a mismatch between an assignment and a person's asserted identity amounted to little more than an incidental case of mistaken ethnic identity. In others, latent prejudice was evident in the assigner's comments, which reflected low expectations for Mexican Americans, even if the assignee appeared to be, in the assigner's mind, an exception to the rule.

That many of the people I spoke with expressed disagreement and even active resistance toward outside expectations about Mexican American identity suggests that Mexican ethnicity, and by extension mestizaje, is still a highly contested area of self- and group identity within the United States. In the next and final chapter we will consider how this current manifestation of American Mestizaje compares with historical precedents and, ultimately, what the past and present may portend for this multiple-generation, most rapidly growing portion of the U.S. population.

6 Imagining Mestizaje in a Sociological Way

At the end of a recent university lecture I gave summarizing the work covered in chapter 4 on intermarriage and social integration, a Latina/o Studies faculty member raised his hand and posed a question that caught me off guard. He asked, essentially, how could I explain the fact that his U.S.–born Mexican American son speaks Spanish well, despite having been raised in a predominantly Anglo midwestern college town? As a point of contrast, he claims that when he goes back to the barrios of his home-town in south Texas, Mexican American kids his son's age and genera-tion barely speak Spanish at all. Not having a ready answer, I stalled by throwing his question back at him. Why did *he* think his son could speak Spanish so well despite living in a town with a relatively low concentration of Mexican Americans?

Not surprisingly, he already knew quite well the answer to his own question. Namely, he and his wife had made deliberate efforts to immerse their son in the Spanish language by speaking it to him at home while he was growing up and making sure he learned it at school. Whereas some middle-class parents might invest considerable time and resources to en-sure their children learn to play piano or violin at an early age, this Latina/o Studies scholar and his wife were determined that their son growing up outside of Aztlan would stay connected to his cultural roots. The irony, as the professor's comments suggest, is that by being middle class, and per-haps even by living in the "American Heartland" far away from the Mexi-can American homeland, his son's acquisition of the Spanish language ap-peared more likely than that of native-born Mexican Americans living in working-class neighborhoods in parts of the Southwest.

Though our exchange was a friendly one, I believe his question was presented as a challenge to my assertion that social structure, as mea-sured by regional factors such as ethnic concentration and social inequal-ity, makes a big difference with regard to the life experiences of Mexican Americans in U.S. society. Despite the national-level evidence I provided that context matters, here was a young man who, against the odds, speaks Spanish well.

Some of my colleagues have tried to assure me this question/comment was not relevant to the lecture. I, however, have tended to interpret it as indicative of a much bigger set of issues. On the one hand, there has been a tendency in Latina/o Studies to give primacy to qualitative methodologies, such as ethnography, case studies, and oral history when looking at ethnic subgroups such as the Mexican-origin population of the United States. This type of work does an excellent job of capturing the cultural richness of being part of a distinct ethnic group within American society, and I myself rely heavily on qualitative methods in my own work.

On the other hand, though there is a good deal of quantitative research in the social sciences that gives a more demographic account of the Mexican-origin population, rarely is an attempt made to tie national-level trends to the subjective experience of ethnic difference and identity transformation. When the "micro/macro connection" is made, the micro focus has usually been on those groups least likely to threaten macro-level categories of race and ethnicity. That is, qualitative community-level research of the Mexican American population usually focuses on first-generation immigrants and their children or later generations living and working in ethnically concentrated environments. There are, of course, good scholarly motivations for taking this approach in the case of Mexican Americans: (a) over two-thirds of Mexican-origin people in the United States are of either the first or second generation; (b) most of this population lives in cities where over a quarter of the population is also of Mexican origin; and (c) as indicated by my own research on intermarriage, there is a tendency for this group to make internal associations with co-ethnics even past the second generation. Thus, placing a qualitative focus on people living in relatively homogeneous ethnic communities is understandable. In doing so, however, we may miss broader trends of integration among Mexican Americans indicated by higher rates of intermarriage over generations and lower levels of housing segregation as individual economic circumstances improve.

Getting Around the "Ecological Fallacy"

Given this conundrum, I believe the Latina/o Studies professor was, in fact, asking precisely the right question: How do national-level trends of social integration relate to individual cases, especially when individual cases appear to contradict national-level trends? A common response to this situation that seemingly leaves everyone off the hook is the claim of the "ecological fallacy." That is, aggregate trends do not make good predictors of individual cases, where innumerable, immeasurable factors contribute to a particular result.[1] For example, though the odds against any one person becoming a successful rock star are extremely high, this statistical reality does not preclude the fact that there are, after all, quite a few successful rock stars in the world whose fates have been shaped by musicianship, ambition, class-privilege, and out-and-out luck, among other things. Conversely, national averages are just that, only averages, and individual exceptions do little to undermine trends found in the aggregate. Though I accept the inherent truth of the ecological fallacy, I also believe it can too easily be employed as a way to not think sociologically. Even if we know there will always be exceptions to a dominant trend, this should not provide us with an excuse for not connecting everyday life to the social and political world at large, or partaking in what C. Wright Mills once defined as the "sociological imagination."[2]

Unfortunately, all too often there appears to be a mutual suspicion between social researchers who do more micro-level qualitative work and those using statistical methods and quantitative data sets. This disconnect between subjective experience and broader societal trends has led to some interesting results, particularly with regard to the way we now think of Latinos in the United States. Richard Rodriguez, for example, probably the most well-known Mexican American author of his generation, has been explicit about his determination not to align his work "with sociology, with sorting, with trading in skins," where "we imagine the point of 'life' is to address some sort of numerical average, common obstacle or persecution."[3] This is a bit disingenuous since he must ultimately be aware that, in the market of ideas, his non-sociological take on life has a particular political sway. His position as a highly regarded Mexican American intellectual assures that his opinions on far-reaching social policies, such as Affirmative Action and bilingual education, will be heard.

In effect, he would like his ideas to have an impact on the aggregate form that constitutes the Mexican American population without having to much concern himself with its specific contours. As detailed in chapter 4, these include a high degree of relative inequality that persists long past the second generation. Rodriguez's eschewing of sociology thus allows him to use his own quite extraordinary biography as evidence that both bilingual education and Affirmative Action programs are inappropriate policies for Mexican Americans that only deepen the cleavages of race and ethnicity in the United States today. Regardless of how one feels about Rodriguez's policy prescriptions (or his considerable talents as a writer, for that matter), his low estimation of sociological methods as a way of getting a grasp on group behavior and aggregate trends in the population must be met with skepticism given his intellectual interest in affecting these very trends.

An additional way that our perceptions of Mexican Americans and other Latinos are shaped through work largely uninformed by the sociological imagination has been well accounted in Arlene Davila's book, *Latinos, Inc.: The Marketing and Making of a People* (2001). In their efforts to satisfy the needs of corporate clientele, Hispanic marketing firms often promote stereotypical or unrealistic representations of U.S. Latinos in their advertising. Hispanic advertising, she argues, attempts to discursively resolve the unfortunate fact (for corporate America) that the most "authentic" Latinos, that is, those with the greatest Spanish-language ability and those with the strongest cultural ties to their country of origin, also tend to have the weakest buying power. As she puts it, "In projecting the idea of the affluent but culture-bound Hispanic, we thus have one of many mélanges that are constructed in the process of selling the market: a construction involving the higher income of the U.S.–born cloaked in the authenticity of the foreign-born, which only becomes apparent when we ignore the intraclass variation among U.S. Latinos."[4]

Hispanic media is thus complicit in the maintenance of a hybrid authentic standard of Latinidad consisting of the cultural and language knowledge of recent immigrants and the affluence of the middle class. Though the business world has an economic interest in comprehending the aggregate trends of this population, marketing pressures to construct a non-threatening, free-spending ethnic consumer preclude the possibility of realistic representation.

How, then, might the underlying theme of this book, mestizaje, help us regain the connection between everyday ethnic experience and the political and social world that in part determines it? That is, how might mestizaje contribute to our development of the sociological imagination? Specifically, in the remainder of this chapter I would like to address how our conceptualization of mestizaje and its particular variation in the United States may help illuminate our understanding of the social structural nature of race and ethnic relations for Mexican Americans today. Before I do that, however, I would like to add some perspective by going back to the

beginning—to the time that mestizaje first mattered to anyone as a meaningful social construct.

Mestizaje in New Spain and Mexico

The *casta* system of race-based social control was established in colonial-
era New Spain. Seventeenth century laws, in what is now Mexico and other
parts of Latin America, sought to regulate multiple aspects of everyday
life. To this end, an elaborate system of status distinctions was imposed on
the population by the colonial government, based on the numerous combinations of Spanish, Indian, and African ancestries. "Social reality, however," as Klor de Alva points out, "did not cooperate."[5] Far from serving
a straightforward descriptive function, the category of mestizo (Spanish-
Indian parentage), and other points along the gradation of official racial
mixing including mulatto (Spanish-African), castizo (Spanish-mestizo),
and morisco (Spanish-mulatto), worked primarily as an ideological basis
for the maintenance of colonial rule. The guiding principal in this hierar-
chical schema was, simply stated, those of pure Spanish descent, especially those born in Spain, were also those best fit to govern.

In seventeenth-century New Spain, then, mestizaje mattered most to
the elite as a way of defining who they were not. One of the key benefits
of this distinction for "pure" Spaniards was the protection it provided from
backbreaking manual labor at a time when famine and epidemics had led
to a dramatic decline in indigenous populations throughout the Americas.[6]
During this period, which also saw considerable economic growth in urban centers and mining, mestizaje ensured that the impact of New World
labor shortages would bypass the Spanish elite and be born instead by
their mixed-race cousins.

But mestizaje from above appeared quite different from mestizaje on
the ground among the mixed and mixing populations of New Spain and
into the period of independence. Cope argues that race mattered comparatively little to the non-elite classes of late seventeenth-century Mexico City
in their day-to-day lives.[7] There, life chances appeared more closely tied to
occupational status and social networks, while official categories of casta
were often appropriated and modified in ways reflecting their increasingly
situational application.

In his population study of the colonial city of Oaxaca, Chance found
that the fluidity of racial classifications permitted many mestizos to pass
as creole, that is, people born in the New World of unmixed Spanish de-

scent. By the eighteenth century these categories had become blurred to the point that mestizo ancestry was granted the status of "purity of blood" *(limpieza de sangre)* in many legal proceedings.[8] In the process of this blurring, creole status shifted from being a category of racial exclusion to one of ethnic nationalism. It was, after all, creole identity, not mestizo identity, that symbolized Mexican independence from Spain, and by the time the official racial classification system was abolished in 1822, it appeared that mestizo status might disappear altogether.[9]

That, of course, is not what happened, and in the Mexican Revolution of the early twentieth century, mestizaje was reborn as the national identity of the Mexican republic. Thus, what began as part of a restrictive scheme to protect political and material resources among Spanish colonists was transformed into a unifying national identity that ostensibly placed great pride in the indigenous contribution to Mexican culture. Through a formulation devised by education minister José Vasconcelos, both political leaders and rural peasants could now claim membership in the "raza cósmica" of Mexican mestizaje.[10] Though the elevation of mestizo and indigenous status in national ideologies may be seen as a positive development, some historians see in the mestizaje of this period primarily a nationalist effort to homogenize a still quite heterogeneous population distinguished in Latin America by severe levels of social inequality between the rich and poor.[11] Thus, mestizaje (not unlike the Latinidad portrayed by Hispanic advertisers) may also be used as a shroud, concealing internal differences of race and culture and the inequitable distribution of power.

Power and the Historical Meanings of Mestizaje

As this brief historical overview reminds us, power itself is a key factor in understanding the specific meaning of mestizaje at a given point in time. In this regard, sociological theory may give us some insight into the relationship among power, social change, and ethnic identity. Through his research on the successes of the Civil Rights Movement, sociologist Doug McAdam developed the political process model, a theoretical way of understanding the role of power in collective actions that result in social change.[12] His approach acknowledges that wealth and power are usually concentrated in the hands of a few elite groups, depriving most people of any real influence over major political decisions. This power disparity, however, is not inevitable. Instead, broad cumulative social processes occasionally open up the opportunity for outside political groups to advance their interests and challenge the status quo. In the case of the Civil Rights Movement, the decline of the U.S. cotton economy; the defeat of fascist regimes during World War II, facilitated in no small part by the participation and heroism of African American troops; and the organizational readiness of black churches and colleges in the South by the 1950s all set the stage for the emergence of the most significant political movement of the twentieth century within the United States.

In their work on racial formation, Omi and Winant expand on the political process model by arguing that identity-based activism during an opportune political moment may also result in challenges to the status quo of race relations. When this happens, a social movement may reformulate social and political conceptions of race and a new social order may emerge.[13] One may thus connect the changing meaning of mestizaje in the Americas over the centuries to the changing political opportunity structure that, by the time of the Mexican Revolution, permitted the transformation of a formerly excluded political class into the master status of the Mexican nation.

In the United States, the most overt expression of mestizo identity came from the direct borrowing of Mexican revolutionary iconography by the Chicano Movement in the late 1960s. Not unlike Mexican intellectuals of the revolutionary period, Chicano activists placed special emphasis on the indigenous side of the mestizo blend, even while their interest in promoting bilingual education betrayed their embrace of the Spanish contribution to Mexican culture, as well. The organizational element of the *Movimiento*, however, appears to have been more directly shaped by factors within the United States. Early leaders of the Raza Unida party in San Antonio, Texas, for example, were inspired by the words and actions of Martin Luther King, Jr., as well as by those of the more politically radical Black Power leader Stokeley Carmichael.[14] Thus, the Chicano Movement in the United States itself represents a compelling hybrid of the mestizo/indigenous iconography of the Mexican Revolution and the political organization lessons of the African American–led Civil Rights Movement.

I would like to argue, however, that the Mexican American experience in the United States has been punctuated by additional variations of mestizaje through the course of the twentieth century and into the present. To help make my point, I include in table 6.1 an ideal typology of the varied forms of mestizaje that have emerged during different political, national, and historical contexts. The rows are categorized along the two primary social structural factors addressed in chapter 4: the relative size of the

Table 6.1 Structural determinants of American Mestizaje

Relative inequality	Political climate	
	Relatively stable	Relatively unstable
	Mestizo majority (Mexico)	
High	Enforced mestizaje— 17th-century New Spain Casta system sets rigid system of racial classification.	Revolutionary mestizaje— Early 20th-century Mexico Mexican Revolution establishes mestizaje as master status of Mexico.
Low	Permeable mestizaje— 18th-century New Spain Racial lines between mestizos and creoles become blurred.	Vanishing mestizaje— Early 19th-century Mexico Creole identity is racially mixed and becomes iconic of Mexican Independence.
	Mestizo minority (United States)	
High	Segmented mestizaje— Early 21st-century United States Mexican Americans are selectively integrated by economic class.	Scapegoat mestizaje— Depression-era United States Half a million Mexican-origin workers are repatriated en masse.
Low	Assimilationist mestizaje— Post–World War II United States Mexican American organizations embrace American ideals.	Reform mestizaje— Vietnam War–Era United States Chicano Movement and ethnic nationalism lead to social reforms.

mestizo population to the dominant population, and the relative level of inequality between mestizos and the dominant group. To give a very general sense for the role of political power in transforming the racial status quo, the columns are divided by periods of relative political stability and periods of relative political instability. During times of political instability, the authority of those in power is called into question and their legitimacy as leaders seriously undermined.

I have included on the top half of table 6.1 categories describing mestizaje in Mexico to draw attention to the historical and geographical continuity of the concept between the United States and Mexico, with the mestizo population of the former being regularly replenished by that of the latter. This also allows me to stress the effect that relative size of the mestizo population has on the specific meaning of mestizaje in different contexts, since mestizos have long constituted the largest portion of the population in what is now Mexico, whereas the Mexican-origin population of the United States is closer to 10 percent.

This is, of course, in many ways a historical comparison that does not give sufficient attention to differences in national political culture, the organization of collective mobilization, the significance of immigrant versus native-born populations, the role of other minority groups, and myriad other factors for which there is not enough space in this chapter or the context of this book to address in a satisfactory manner. However, the point is not to provide a comprehensive historical overview. Rather, we will consider here the different manifestations this ambiguous term has had in different times and places with the goal of ultimately imbuing mestizaje with the specific meaning it too often lacks in popular usage.

The top left cell of table 6.1 is characterized by a large, mixed-race population, relative political stability, and high levels of social inequality between mestizos and the dominant population. This typifies the rigid casta system of late seventeenth-century New Spain. Though there is now evidence that non-elite classes were able to manipulate the casta system within limits, and that there was emerging a degree of ambiguity with regard to what racial subcategory a given individual fell into, colonial law worked to maintain strict distinctions and regulate social status on the basis of race.

Eighteenth-century New Spain saw an increase in the relative and absolute size of the mestizo population and, at least in parts of what would become Mexico, a decrease in inequality between creoles and mestizos. It is thus perhaps not surprising that Chance found evidence that many mestizos assimilated, both through intermarriage and social mobility, into creoles.[15] By this time, racial status had become more porous and tied to factors such as occupation and cultural assimilation. This period of relative political stability provides the basis for permeable mestizaje.

The political instability brought on by the weakening of colonial rule and the drive for Mexican independence from Spain led to a point at the beginning of the nineteenth century where, Chance argues, the category of mestizo became almost irrelevant. The official system of racial classification was dismantled, and the iconic patriot of Mexican independence was the now racially mixed category of the creole. Mestizo assimilation and the irrelevance of the category for creoles in power contributed to the period characterized here by vanishing mestizaje.

High levels of social inequality make revolutionary mestizaje similar structurally to enforced mestizaje, with the exception that dominant group power is undermined, thus contributing to a period of political instability. In the case of the Mexican Revolution, the collapse of the de-legitimized regime of Porfirio Diaz opened the path for political revolution through the organized uprising of the impoverished mestizo majority.[16] Here, the historically subordinate status of mestizo is inverted and becomes institutionalized as the racial and cultural standard for the nation.

In considering a context where mestizos constitute a comparatively small portion of the national population, we move to the United States. If we begin in the category where inequality between the mestizo population and the dominant group, in this case Anglos, is relatively high during a time of political stability, we find a good match with the present period of what might be referred to as segmented mestizaje. Though there is a degree of social mobility experienced by Mexican Americans, compared to other groups, their levels of educational and occupational attainment across generations remain relatively low. As the present study shows, for those who have attained higher levels of socioeconomic mobility, there are higher levels of social integration as measured by intermarriage. Thus, in a society highly stratified by social class, such as the United States today, Mexican Americans are, to a large degree, selectively integrated with the dominant group on the basis of their class status. More broadly, there may, in fact, be mainstream acceptance of Latinos in the context of segmented mestizaje, but their representation in popular culture often stresses the idealized middle-class segment described by Davila, in *Latinos, Inc.*

A similar structural situation, but under relative political instability, may lead to a situation marked by scapegoat mestizaje. When Mexican Americans make up a clear minority of the population and experience a high degree of social inequality during a time when political leadership is called into question, they may find themselves the object of scapegoat politics. One of the most egregious examples of this during the twentieth century was repatriation during the Great Depression, when some 500,000 Mexican-origin people living in the United States were either pressured into returning or forcibly deported to Mexico.[17] Immigrant scapegoating appears to be an ongoing feature of the U.S. political landscape, as is made clear at the national level in the anti-immigrant provisions of both the Illegal Immigration Act and the Welfare Reform Act passed by Congress in

1996, and at the state level in recent years by the popular support for vindictive anti-immigration legislation such as Proposition 187 in California and Proposition 200 in Arizona.[18] Still, we may expect immigrant scapegoating to be especially salient during times of high Mexican American/Anglo inequality and relative political instability.[19]

It is generally agreed among social demographers that the middle part of the twentieth century, from the 1960s to the early 1970s, experienced one of the most equitable distributions of economic resources in U.S. history. Since 1973, in fact, social inequality has increased, with Latinos as a group being hit particularly hard, largely due to their low average levels of educational attainment.[20]

In contrast, the first two decades of the post-war period saw dramatic growth in the size of the U.S. middle class and what might be described as assimilationist mestizaje among Mexican Americans. As discussed in chapter 3, assimilationist ideals were evident in the goals of voluntary organizations such as the LULAC and the G.I. Forum. These groups contributed greatly to the early success of the Civil Rights Movement by providing mobilization support for desegregation in the Southwest and the equal application of constitutional rights for all Americans regardless of race or ethnicity. The thrust of their politics, not unlike that of the early Civil Rights Movement as a whole, emphasized their embrace of the American ideals of liberty and equality before the law.[21]

Near the end of this period of relatively low social inequality, the authority of the American government was severely undermined by its drawn-out participation in the Vietnam War, as well as by the sense that assimilationist politics were not sufficiently addressing the long-term societal cleavages established by American race ideology. Again, compared to what had come before and, in fact, compared to the present time, this was a period of historically low social inequality. This fact, combined with the political instability of the late 1960s and early 1970s, set the stage for the emergence of the reform mestizaje of the Chicano and other nationalist movements of the period. Though the Chicano Movement borrowed directly from the iconography of the Mexican Revolution and led to events that were violent and even deadly, it did not result in a social revolution. Instead, it was met by the Anglo majority in power with selected reforms in the treatment of Mexican Americans and other U.S. minority groups also engaged at the time in the politics of ethnic nationalism.[22]

Mestizaje and Official Categories of Race and Ethnicity in the United States

One aspect of these reforms was the congealing of what David Hollinger refers to as the "ethno-racial pentagon," that is, the official classifications of race and ethnicity established by Directive 15 of the Federal Office of Management and the Budget (OMB).[23] This system, used by the U.S. Census Bureau and other data-collecting government agencies, was a direct offshoot of the Civil Rights Era triad of federal laws—the Voting Rights Act of 1965, the Civil Rights Act of 1964, and the Housing Act of 1968—which require that we know the ethnic make-up of the population. That is, the only way we can be sure whether things like housing or occupational discrimination do or do not exist is if we have some way of measuring race and ethnic differences in the population. To accomplish this, Directive 15 of the OMB divided the United States into four categories of race—white, Asian American, African American, and Native American—and four categories of Hispanic ethnicity—Mexican origin, Cuban American, Puerto Rican, and other.

In recent years this system has come under attack from various points on the political spectrum. Though there are surely many people who would prefer to get rid of these categories as a way of creating overnight a "color-blind" society, much of the demand for their reformulation before the 2000 census came from individuals and organizations who felt the categories no longer matched reality. There are simply too many people of mixed racial and ethnic background for the categories, set as they were, to provide a valid account of the population at large.[24] No doubt, the limits placed on individual freedom of self-identification played a central role in the call for change, as well.

One population that, as a group, has been particularly resistant to buying into the U.S. classification system of race and ethnicity is U.S. Latinos. In pretests leading up to the 2000 census, Latinos were the most likely to respond as "other" in the race category, or to simply not follow the survey's directions, checking more than one box even when instructed not to do so.[25] As some of the interviews in this study have highlighted, mestizaje, even in its contemporary form in the United States, remains ambiguous, situationally flexible, and, at least in the context of government surveys, an uneasy fit in the officially sanctioned classificatory system of race and ethnicity.

While many quantitative researchers have continued to scratch their heads over how to clearly define the Latino population, scholars working in the areas of Latina/o studies, anthropology, and social history have for many years been addressing the ambiguous, contested, and creative nature of Latino identity in the United States. Gloria Anzaldúa's *Border-lands/La Frontera: The New Mestiza* (1987) represents a kind of water-shed in this respect, paving the way for the deluge of social research that uses the Southwest borderland as both a site of empirical fieldwork and metaphor for the "internal borderlands" that shape Latino lives and iden-tities through day-to-day interactions with others in U.S. society.[26] This framework stresses the centrality of contradictions and ambiguity within Latino identity, while acknowledging the persistent constraints imposed on Latinidad through patriarchy, social inequality, and the demands of global capitalism. A point of primary importance in much of this work is the socioeconomic position held by Latinos in U.S. society, employed dis-proportionately in the low-wage service sector and marked as culturally, and often racially, distinct.

To their credit, sociologists have undertaken research crucial to our understanding of demographic trends within the Latino population and La-tino social history, and a few researchers have begun to consider the social structural factors that shape Latino identity.[27] It is striking, however, that at this moment in time—not long after the 2000 census when most demog-raphers are aware of the survey problems associated with identifying the Latino population—little effort has been made to connect the enthusiasm for understanding ambiguity and the internal borderlands of self-identity in Latina/o Studies with the inadequacy of the current official system of race and ethnic categories.

Categorical Ambiguity and the Need for Specificity

The reluctance to deal head-on with the ambiguous nature of mestizaje in sociology rests, I believe, on an unspoken, if unfounded, assumption: an admission of categorical ambiguity will tend to undermine the progressive political potential of Latino identity. Somehow the admission of internal differences will contribute to the "divide and conquer" strategies of con-servative politics. The risk that Latino identity may be used for politically conservative ends seems real enough. In their analysis of a national sur-vey of Latino politics, De la Garza et al. found that the majority of Cuban Americans, Mexican Americans, and Puerto Ricans in each group identify ideologically as moderate to conservative. There is also clear evidence that the George W. Bush–led Republican Party is keen on gaining Latino political support.[28] It is not clear, however, that acknowledging categorical ambiguity works against the viability of progressive Latino politics. If anything, it is the lack of specificity with regard to social inequality, regional differences in ethnic concentration, and cultural changes related to ongoing immigration and generations spent in the United States that permits, for example, Hispanic marketing firms to misrepresent Latinos in their ad campaigns and politically conservative writers to argue that, across the board, Affirmative Action policies and bilingual education programs do not serve the interest of the Latino population.

In a sense, the crux of the problem lies within the strategic use of categorical ambiguity. Categorical ambiguity is itself the product of a large population and the bureaucratic need to track it, such that smaller groups of people from diverse backgrounds may fall under one overarching category such as Latino. The categorical ambiguity of Latinidad (or Mexicanidad, for that matter) can thus be used strategically to obfuscate internal differences of class, gender, race, and generation. This, I would argue, is an inherently conservative maneuver that, depending on the political moment, allows those with political influence to depict subgroups within the population as primarily a cost ("they" are not like us and threaten our way of life) or benefit ("they" are enough like us to help perpetuate our way of life) to the rest of society. Even from the more "radical" position of ethnic nationalism, the strategic use of categorical ambiguity often implies a willingness to engage in a conservative form of politics that espouses some fixed cultural standard as an ideal.

In contrast, a more progressive strategy would use categorical ambiguity as a starting point from which to specify historical context and the various sources of social inequality and difference that demarcate categories, such as Latino and Mexican American, to begin with. My use of mestizaje as an underlying theme in this study has sought to do just that. An important outcome of this approach has been to acknowledge a remarkably obvious fact. Namely, the Mexican-origin population (and that of other non-European-origin populations, including Chinese, Filipino, and Japanese) has had a lengthy history in the United States that, for many members of this group, dates back to or precedes the mass arrival of European immigrants in the United States during the late 1800s and early 1900s. Popular and scholarly accounts that depict U.S. Latinos and Asians as "new immigrants" fail to acknowledge this history, and they discount the diversity of experiences within these highly heterogeneous populations. That said, there is considerable evidence, especially with regard to educational attainment, that social inequality is a persistent problem past the second generation for the largest of these groups, Mexican Americans. It is only through the disaggregation of this population by generation, however, that this becomes apparent. An accurate assessment of the status of groups with high rates of current immigration requires, at the very least, specificity with regard to generation.

Out of the Ethnic Present and into the American Future

By specifying Mexican Americans whose families have been here for at least three generations, the present study has taken an unusual strategy. It draws our attention to the reasons Mexican ethnicity tends to endure, even after a family's direct experience of immigration from Mexico has faded from memory. In this respect, four interrelated factors stand out. First, the concentration of Mexican Americans in the Southwest and California underlies all other explanations for the robustness of Mexican ethnicity. In these regions of the country, the average Mexican American lives in a city where approximately a third of the population is also of Mexican descent, a proportion that increases the closer one gets to the international border. That this large and growing population is also marked by low levels of educational attainment only works to accentuate the distinctiveness of Mexican Americans from the majority population.

A second factor directly stemming from the first is the symbolic context of Mexican ethnicity. Melting into the mainstream, a contentious notion to begin with, is not an obvious path when so much of local culture—whether gleaned through the electronic media, on the streets, or at home with family—reflects the geographic and social proximity to Mexico. A good critique of "mainstream culture" might, in fact, begin with an acknowledgment of the many outside streams, including Latino culture, that perpetually modify it.

Third, the critical mass of Mexican Americans found in cities such as Phoenix and San Jose allows for forms of ethnic organization that would not otherwise be possible. Even Mexican American professionals who work in predominantly Anglo work environments can find a degree of ethnic solidarity by joining ethnic identity professional organizations. Motivations for joining the Society of Hispanic Professional Engineers or Chicanos por la Causa, to give two examples, are myriad. A common theme among the professional "joiners" I interviewed, however, was a desire to be involved with and give back to the Mexican American community through tutoring, coaching, and other volunteer activities. Even if the confrontational Chicano activism of the 1960s and 1970s has waned in recent decades, the spirit of that era persists in the willingness of Mexican Americans to volunteer in organizations that acknowledge their debt to the past through work done in the predominantly working-class ethnic community.

A final factor key to understanding the durable nature of Mexican ethnicity is the perception of Mexican ethnicity by outside groups. As described above, the present relationship between the majority population and Mexican Americans is marked by what I call segmented mestizaje. A way of understanding this is to view it as a kind of selective tolerance of ethnic difference on the basis of class. So long as Mexican Americans are able to attain middle-class status through a college education and employment in white-collar jobs, they are likely to find themselves in integrated environments with friends and acquaintances of different backgrounds. Intermarriage patterns closely tied to levels of education reflect this fact.

Once accepted as peers, however, many of the people I spoke with encountered, often to their surprise, negative attitudes towards Mexican ethnicity among their coworkers. Sometimes this was couched in the language of "reverse discrimination," while other times low expectations and stereotypes were betrayed in the surprise that a coworker expressed upon discovering a professional Mexican American in the workplace. "You don't seem Mexican," is the phrase that probably captures best the incongruity of accepting a person's class status while being caught off guard by her ethnicity. Though the people I interviewed tended to have strong opinions about the nature of their ethnicity and their reasons for identifying the way they do, they nonetheless occasionally found themselves in situations where their self-identity conflicted with the expectations of that identity by others.

If segmented mestizaje seems like a drag on the unhindered expression of Mexican ethnicity, it pales alongside the vindictiveness of scapegoat mestizaje. When inequality is high and economically troubled times threaten to undermine the legitimacy of those in power, ethnic and immigrant scapegoating can become an attractive political option. The passage of Proposition 200 in Arizona during the November 2004 election and the homegrown patriotism manifest in the volunteer troops of "minuteman militia" stationed along the U.S.–Mexico border in the spring of 2005 suggest that a strategy of blaming the relatively powerless for the economic insecurity of U.S. workers may once again be gaining popular support.[29]

A potentially important damper on scapegoat politics is the growing influence of non-immigrant Mexican Americans. Though by a small margin, a majority of Mexican Americans in Arizona disapproved of Proposition 200 and, as noted at the end of chapter 1, college campuses have seen a new generation of students spurred to political action in opposition to this initiative.[30] More recently in California, anti-immigrant rhetoric coming from the governor's office has been met with a cool reception by Latinos, who now make up one of every five members of the state Legislature and count among their ranks the mayors of both Los Angeles and San Jose.[31] Though it is never wise to presume Latino support for "Latino" issues, such as liberal immigration policy and bilingual education, the increasing participation of Mexican Americans in the democratic process is encouraging and helps lessen the division between those in power and those not in power along the lines of race and ethnicity. The central irony here is that, over the past ten years or so, scapegoat politics itself has likely been an important motivator for Mexican Americans to show up in higher numbers at the polls.

The future of American Mestizaje is thus, as always, uncertain. But history suggests that the size of the Mexican-origin population, its access to political power, and the degree of inequality it experiences in relation to the majority population will strongly determine the extent and quality of integration it attains within American society. The array of possible outcomes ranges from a return to the era of repatriation, in which millions of undocumented workers and their families are deported while native-born Mexican Americans stand by unable or unwilling to intervene, to a more virtuous scenario in which third- and fourth-generation Mexican Americans and Americans of all backgrounds see in the lives of the first generation a common history of striving and the struggle for better opportunities.

This last possibility has interesting implications. First, it contains the seed of hope that out of the recognition of a shared humanity will emerge immigration policies that acknowledge the contributions of immigrants, legal or not, to American society and treat them accordingly in a humane fashion. Second, it would seem that the moment most Americans recognize their common bond with immigrants of diverse class and cultural backgrounds will be the moment the word mestizaje no longer applies only to people of Mexican or Latino heritage. Rather, it will refer to the enduring process of racial and cultural mixing that the United States has long shared with the rest of the Americas.

Mestizaje, as it turns out, does not end at Mexico's frontier with the United States. Beneath official categories of race and ethnicity, it has maintained a subterranean existence, though the signs are everywhere that it will soon come out into the light of day. When it does, America will not so much change, in fact, as its people will have to face the reality of the country's complicated history and the profoundly interdependent relationships of those who live within it.

Appendix I

Selected Respondent Attributes

Name	Age	Ethnicity	Generation
Phoenix metro area sample			
Chuck	45	Mexican American	3rd
Neil	36	Mexican American, Irish	3rd
Andy	25	Mexican American	3rd and 4th
Jerry	38	Mexican American	3rd
Claudia	35	Mexican American	4th
Mario	26	Mexican American	2nd and 4th
Teresa	35	Mexican American	3rd and 4th
Leo	38	Mexican American	4th
Trina	38	Mexican American	2nd and 3rd
Felipe	30	Mexican American	2nd and 3rd
Phil	35	Mexican American/Chicano	3rd and 4th
Ed	28	Chicano	4th
Janet	25	Mexican American, Filipino	4th
Vicki	37	Mexican American	4th
Sylvia	40	Mexican American, Basque	3rd
Gloria	25	Mexican American, Spanish, English, Irish, German	3rd and native
David	27	Mexican American, English	4th
Eva	29	Chicana	4th
Michael	38	Mexican American	4th
Rick	31	Chicano	3rd and 4th
Brad	27	Mexican American, Spanish, German, Irish	5th
Mayra	34	Mexican American, white	3rd
Alex	31	Hispanic, Lithuanian, Spanish	4th
Susie	34	Mexican American, Polish, German, English	3rd
Mary	29	Mexican American, white	4th
Elena	36	Mexican American	2nd and 3rd

Education	Occupation
BS	Engineer
Some college	Air and rescue communication specialist
BA	Clerk, boat shop
BS	Administrator, non-profit
MA	Planning director, non-profit
Some college	Shipping and receiving clerk
MA	City council staffer
Some college	Flight attendant
BS	Marketing manager
Some College	Firefighter
BA	Hispanic marketing manager
Some college	Corporate consultant
BA	Public relations
MA	High school math teacher
Some college	Electrical designer
BA	Advertising account executive
Some college	Computer programming student
MA	Domestic violence counselor
BA	Mortgage investment administrator
BA	Assignment editor
MA	Law student
BA	Production scheduler
Some college	Internet business owner
BA	Government accountant
BA	Grade school teacher
Some college	Shipping analyst

Name	Age	Ethnicity	Generation
San Jose metro area sample			
Carol	41	Greek, American Indian, French, Mexican American	4th
John	37	Mexican American	4th
Allen	31	Mexican American	3rd and 4th
Joe	35	Mexican American	3rd
Cara	26	Mexican, Irish, German	3rd
Val	35	Mexican American, Swedish	3rd
Bernard	27	Chicano, Swedish	3rd
Ken	30	Mexican, white, Filipino	4th
Margaret	33	Mexican American	3rd and native
Dan	37	Chicano, Comanche	4th
Angie	27	Mexican American	3rd
Rachel	25	Mexican American, English, Irish, Scottish	3rd
Vera	32	Mexican American, German	3rd
Bob	30	Mexican American, Italian, Russian	3rd
Gary	37	Mexican American, German	native
Lydia	25	Chicana	3rd and 4th
Keith	34	Mexican American	3rd
Carolyn	37	Mexican American	3rd
Andrea	28	Mexican American	3rd
Henry	31	Chicano/Mexican American, Irish, German	3rd and native
Rosemarie	38	Chicana	3rd and 4th
Roberto	43	Chicano	2nd and 3rd
Jenny	26	Mexican American	2nd and 4th
Ted	40	Mexican American	3rd

Education	Occupation
Some college	Personal trainer
BS	Technology consultant
BS	Health and safety specialist
BA	Public relations
BA	Job recruiter
BS	Rates analyst
BA	Financial analyst
MBA	Financial analyst
Some college	Administrative assistant
BS	Hardware engineer
BA	Business school student
MS	Environmental engineer
BA	High school math teacher
BA	Junior high English teacher
BA	Surfboard shop owner
BS	Marketing engineer
BA	University outreach program director
BA	Billing clerk
Some college	Administrative assistant
Law degree	Attorney
MA	University instructor
BA	Youth group coordinator
BS	Product manager
BA	Software company vice president

Appendix II

Third-Plus-Generation Mexican American Interview Schedule

The interview begins with question #5 of the 2000 census, which concerns the respondent's Hispanic ethnicity (fig. A.1). Respondents are then asked to name which of the three Mexican-origin identities given (Mexican, Mexican American, Chicano) they most strongly identify with.

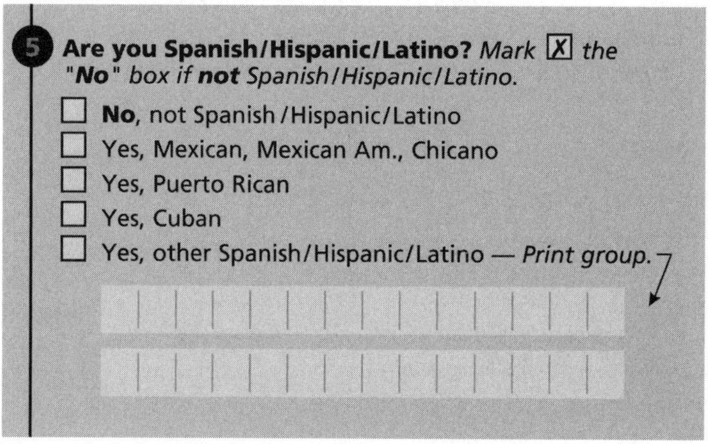

5 Are you Spanish/Hispanic/Latino? *Mark* X *the* "**No**" *box if* **not** *Spanish/Hispanic/Latino.*

☐ **No**, not Spanish/Hispanic/Latino
☐ Yes, Mexican, Mexican Am., Chicano
☐ Yes, Puerto Rican
☐ Yes, Cuban
☐ Yes, other Spanish/Hispanic/Latino — *Print group.*

Figure A.1 Question #5 from 2000 census regarding respondent's ethnicity

The interview then proceeds with the following schedule.

Personal Information

1. Where were you born?
2. Where did you grow up?
3. How long have you lived where you live now?
4. How old are you?
5. What is your occupation?
6. What is the highest level of education you have attained?
7. Did you attend a public or private grade school/high school?

Family History

8. Who in your family originally migrated from Mexico?
9. What part of Mexico did they come from?
10. How long ago did they first arrive in the United States?
11. Why did they leave Mexico?
12. Where did they originally settle?
13. What was their occupation?
14. What was the level of education they had attained when they arrived in the United States?
15. How do you know this information?
16. Where were your parents born?
17. What is their occupation?
18. What is the highest level of education they have attained?
19. Where do they live now?
20. Do you maintain regular contact with your parents and/or siblings?

Ethnic Context

21. About what percentage of the local population where you grew up was of Mexican ancestry?
22. How did you consider yourself ethnically/racially when you were growing up?
23. Of what ethnicity/race were most of your friends growing up?
24. How did your parents feel about your Mexican-origin background?
25. What is your parents' first language?
26. Did your parents speak Spanish to you or to each other when you were growing up?
27. Did they ever discuss their choice of language usage with you?
28. Did they belong to any organizations or clubs, ethnic or not?
29. Was it important to your parents that you date someone who was ethnically Mexican?
30. Did or would your parents approve of you marrying someone who was not of Mexican ancestry?

Cultural Practices

31. Do you regularly eat Mexican food? What is your favorite? Can you prepare Mexican food? If so, how did you learn to do this?
32. What religion were your parents when you were growing up? What religion are you presently? Do you attend services regularly?

33. Are there any holidays that your family celebrates that you associate with your Mexican heritage? What about these holidays seems particularly Mexican?

34. If you have children, how important is their Mexican/Mexican American/Chicana/o identity to them?

35. Would you prefer your children marry someone who also has Mexican ancestry? Why?

36. Do you speak Spanish? If so, in what contexts do you usually speak it? How did you learn to speak it? If you do not speak Spanish, can you understand it?

37. Are there any Spanish language programs on television that you watch regularly? If so, what are they and why do you watch them?

38. Do you listen to Latin music? If so, what artists do you like and why? When and how did you first get interested in Latin music?

39. Are there any other customs or practices you can think of that affect your day-to-day life that you associate with your Mexican heritage?

Ethnic Identity

40. Is being Mexican/Mexican American/Chicana/o important to you?

41. Do you belong to any organizations, ethnic or not?

42. Are you married?

43. If so, what is the ethnicity/race of your spouse?

44. Of what ethnic group are your friends?

45. Of what ethnic group are your co-workers?

46. What is the most common ethnic/racial group in the neighborhood where you presently live?

47. Do you feel more comfortable around people of Mexican ancestry than other people? Why?

48. What kind of contact do you have with first-generation immigrants?

49. Do you maintain contact with relatives or friends in Mexico? How often do you see or communicate with them?

50. Have you ever been to Mexico? If so, what was that experience like?

51. Do you think there are some social traits common to people of Mexican ancestry? What are they? Do you feel you exhibit them?

52. Do you think there are some social traits common to U.S. citizens? What are they? Do you exhibit these traits?

53. Is it common for people to ask you about your ethnic identity? What are these interactions like? How do you feel about them?

54. How do you feel about bilingual education in U.S. schools?

55. How do you feel about current Affirmative Action policy?
56. How do you feel about Mexican immigration into the United States?
57. On the whole, do you believe it is advantageous or disadvantageous to be identified as being of Mexican ancestry? Why?
58. Do you have any additional comments or questions about the interview? Thank you for your time.

Appendix III

Sample Selection and Interview Procedures

In Phoenix, I began by speaking with an administrator in a large non-profit organization that is broadly connected to both the private and non-profit sectors. My goal was to begin with an organization that was not an ethnic identity organization, but which I knew had Mexican Americans on staff. After I made my initial contact and interviews there, I branched out to interview professional, social, and familial contacts given to me by the first batch of interviewees. This worked quite well for me in Phoenix, though I had less success with this approach in the San Francisco Bay area.

There, after a month of no responses from non-profits, I decided I would try contacting a few Hispanic identity professional organizations, including one aimed primarily at Hispanics in business—broadly defined—and an organization of Hispanic engineers, a significant group in the Silicon Valley. Near the end of my stay in that region, I also placed an ad in the bulletin for a Catholic church in East San Jose, a region where there are many immigrants from a variety of origins, including the Philippines, Vietnam, Central America, and Mexico. I was able to send my announcement out on e-mail lists for three organizations, which proved advantageous since it was ultimately distributed and forwarded beyond the original recipients, and the announcement enabled me to interview people working in education, environmental safety, and journalism, as well. The central difference, then, between the two samples is that in the Phoenix area, I deliberately did not select interviewees through ethnic identity organizations, whereas, in the San Jose region, I did. For a summary of interviewee characteristics, please refer to Appendix I.

A major concern in a study like this is that many people may have chosen to participate in the project because of their strong ethnic sentiment to begin with. It is notable, for example, that only one interviewee, who, not coincidentally, was only part Mexican, did not at the time of the interview self-identify using any Mexican-origin identity. Despite my efforts to include people for whom ethnicity held little importance, I found it particularly difficult to find Mexican-origin people who generally self-identified without reference to their Mexican background. Moreover, that I did not hide the fact that the interview concerned third-plus-generation social integration and that I myself am third-generation Mexican American likely contributed to an interview setting in which ethnicity was a more salient factor than it would have been otherwise. That said, I do believe the interviewees' knowledge of my own ethnicity permitted a degree of frankness, especially when concerning unfair treatment and the assignment of ethnic identity by Anglos, that otherwise might not have been obtained.

Once a participant was recruited, a one- to three-hour tape-recorded interview was arranged, depending on the interviewee's availability, at his/her place of work or residence. I began the interview by showing the participant a copy of the year 2000 U.S. census and asking how s/he answered or would have answered question #5, which asks if the respondent is Spanish/Hispanic/Latino or not. An interview schedule was then followed, which revolves around the central theme of social integration (see Appendix II).

Appendix IV

Methodological Appendix for Chapter 4

The Current Population Survey (CPS) follows a 4-8-4 rotation cycle through which a household is interviewed at monthly intervals for four months (e.g., January through April), goes eight months without being interviewed, and then reenters the sample for four more months of interviews (e.g., January through April). To avoid redundant cases, every other year of the survey was used. Cases were restricted to those individuals living within Metropolitan Statistical Areas (MSAs) where there were sufficient cases in the CPS data to construct the structural variables described below. These selection criteria yielded 1,996 husbands and 2,485 wives. All selected cases were weighted with CPS weights, which approximate the size of the national population, and then deflated back to the number of cases actually selected so as to maintain proportionality without distorting measures of statistical significance.

Problems of Selection

Two problems in the selection of cases are immediately evident. First, the fact of intermarriage means there will be and already are a good number of people of mixed Mexican/non-Mexican background, and it is by no means clear how these people self-identify ethnically in surveys such as the CPS. If, for example, there is a tendency for people of part Mexican ancestry married to Anglos to identify themselves as Anglos, then we will have underestimated Mexican-origin/Anglo intermarriage. On the other hand, it may be that the popularity of identity politics has made it more acceptable, or perhaps desirable, to self-identify as an ethnic or racial minority, in which case we may be overestimating intermarriage by including people of mixed ancestry who, by some standard, might not normally "count" as Mexican American. Currently, there is no reliable way of predicting either bias.

Second, the selective migration of respondents within the United States means we must use caution when interpreting the effects of region and structural variables such as ethnic concentration, group size, and percent foreign-born. Certain regions of the country may indeed be more conducive to the social integration of Mexican Americans with other Americans. *Or,* people who are already well integrated may be the ones most likely to move to these regions to begin with. This is a difficult issue to get around without specific information about the place of marriage, though the fact that there are long-standing Mexican American communities in places such as Chicago, Missouri, and the Pacific Northwest, often connected to the routes of migrant farming, suggests that social integration is by no means a prerequisite for living outside the more ethnically concentrated regions of the Southwest and California. The inclusion of the region variable in the models described below should also capture, to some extent, the effect of broadly defined geographical preferences for more assimilated respondents, if such preferences in fact exist.

Variable Definitions

The dichotomous dependent variable is marriage to a Mexican American versus marriage to a non-Hispanic white. Education is specified in the regression models as a categorical variable consisting of the following categories: less than a high school diploma, high school graduation, some college, and bachelor's degree. First-generation respondents consist of those who were not born in the United States, the second generation is defined as those who were born in the United States but have at least one foreign-born parent, and the third-plus generation consists of all U.S.–born respondents whose parents were both born in the United States, as well. Regions were defined as follows: Texas (reference category), Southwest (Arizona, Colorado, and New Mexico), California, and Other Regions (the rest of the United States).

Structural variables were also pooled from the 1994–2002 Outgoing Rotation of the CPS and then linked to individual-level cases by MSA. Only those MSAs containing at least twenty Mexican-origin cases over the age of twenty in the pooled sample were used. In all, the structural file contained 1,092,070 cases, 8.5 percent of which consisted of people of Mexican-origin living in 141 MSAs in forty states.

The sex ratio was derived by dividing the number of Mexican-origin males between the ages of fifteen and sixty by like females in the sample from each MSA, such that a value greater than one indicates more men than women, and a value less than one indicates more women than men in the population. Status inequality is simply the mean over-twenty educational attainment of Anglos divided by that of the Mexican-origin population, such that a number higher than one indicates inequality in the favor of Anglos. Internal status diversity was calculated by deriving the M6 diversity index of educational attainment in each MSA for the Mexican-origin population over age twenty, such that the higher the value of the index, the higher the level of internal status diversity within the Mexican-origin population.

Status inequality and internal status diversity are based on a seven-point scale of educational attainment, where one equals less than a ninth-grade education, two equals a ninth- though twelfth-grade education without a high school diploma, three equals high school graduation, four equals some college, five equals an associate's degree, six equals a bachelor's degree, and seven equals an advanced degree. Status inequality between Mexican Americans and Anglos is calculated by simply dividing the Anglo educational attainment average in a given MSA by the Mexican-origin average in the same metro area. Status parity between Anglos and Mexican Americans would be reflected in a value of 1.0 for this variable. Any number greater than 1.0 would indicate status inequality in the favor of Anglos who, on average, tend to have higher levels of educational attainment than Mexican Americans. The M6 diversity index for educational attainment among the Mexican-origin population is calculated as follows:

$$Nc \left[1 \leftrightarrow ((\Sigma \mid Xij \leftrightarrow Xi \mid) / 2) / \Sigma \, Xij\right],$$

where Nc is the number of educational categories containing at least one person in MSA i, Xij is the number of people in MSA i and educational category j, and Xi is the mean number of people across educational categories in MSA i. (See Jack P. Gibbs and Dudley L. Poston Jr. 1975. "The Division of Labor: Conceptualization and Related Measures," *Social Forces* 53: 468–476.)

Relative group size is measured using Mexican ethnic concentration, that is, the number of Mexican-origin cases divided by the total number of cases in each MSA. Percent foreign-born is the number of foreign-born Mexican immigrants divided by the total number of the Mexican-origin cases in each MSA.

Notes

Chapter 1

1. Klor de Alva, 1996, 67.

2. See, for example, Bean and Tienda, 1987; Fox, 1996; Olmos, Ybarra and Monterrey, 1999; Suro, 1998; Shorris, 1992; and Suarez-Orozco and Paez, 2002.

3. See, for example, Alba et al., 1999; Chiswick and Sullivan, 1995; Massey, 1985; and Qian, 1997.

4. See Alba, 1985; Alba, 1990; Gans, 1979; Lieberson and Waters, 1988; Neidert and Farley, 1985; and Waters, 1990.

5. See Tuan, 1998, for an important challenge to this tendency through an examination of the persistence of Asian identity past the second generation among Japanese and Chinese Americans living in California.

6. See Alba and Nee, 1997; Perlmann and Waldinger, 1997; Portes and Rumbaut, 2001; Rumbaut, 1997; and Zhou, 1997.

7. Consejo Nacional de Población, 2001, 4.

8. The classic statement of how group size, stratification, and diversity relate to social integration is made in Blau, 1977.

9. See Cornell and Hartmann, 1998; Espiritu, 1992; Garcia, 1997; Nagel, 1996; and Omi and Winant, 1994.

10. See, for example, Collins, 1989; Durr and Logan, 1997; and Grodsky and Pager, 2001.

11. Blau, 1977, 265–266; and Anderson and Saenz, 1994, 414–430.

12. De la Garza et al., 1992, 25.

13. Alba et al., 1999, 451.

14. Massey and Denton, 1992, 256.

15. See Alba, 1990; and Waters, 1990.

16. Bean et al., 2001, 256.

17. See Qian, 1997; and Qian, 1999.

18. Gonzales, 1999, 114–117.

19. Gonzales, 1999, 118.

20. Barrera, 1979; and Blauner, 1979, 83.

21. Dimas, 1999, 23.

22. Gonzales, 1999, 132.

23. Barrera, 1979, 88.

24. Barrera, 1979, 91.

25. Dimas, 1999, 23.

26. Luckingham, 1994, 33.

27. Luckingham, 1994, 40.

28. Luckingham, 1994, 50.

29. Pitti, 2003, 12.

30. Pitti, 2003, 13.

31. Pitti, 2003, 17.

32. Pitti, 2003, 23.

33. Almaguer, 1992; and Barrera, 1979.

34. Wollenberg, 1985, 264.

35. Luckingham, 1994, 51.

36. Rodriguez, 1999, 75.

37. Ibid.

38. Luckingham, 1994, 60.

39. Ibid.

40. Ibid.

41. Dimas, 1999, Ch. 3.

42. Billeaud, "Prop. 200 Won Support from Blue-collar Workers," *Associated Press*, November 3, 2004.

43. Cooper, "High Noon on the Border," *The Nation,* June 6, 2005; and Adams, "Proposition 187 Lessons," *Z Magazine,* March 1995.

44. "Latino Voting in California Surged in 1996 Election," *Los Angeles Times,* December 31, 1997

45. Wingett, "Younger Latinos React to Prop. 200: New Generation of Activist Born," *Arizona Republic,* December 12, 2004.

46. Ibid.

Chapter 2

1. Anderson, 1983.

2. See, for example, Bankston and Henry, 1999; Chavez, 1994; Donner, 2001; Hackenberg and Benequista, 2001; Jacobs, 2002; and Malkki, 1995.

3. Anderson, 1983, 6.

4. Giddens, 1991, 2–5, 23–27.

5. Davila, 2001, 69.

6. Given the preference among Latinos to self-identify using national-origin identities over pan-ethnic identities, it is not altogether clear how effective Spanish-language media has been in producing Latino or Hispanic identity, either. In this regard, see De la Garza et al., 1992, 13; and Oboler, 1995.

Chapter 3

1. Garcia, 1997, Ch. 6; and Nagel, 1996, 121–141.

2. Gordon, 1964, 71.

3. Gordon, 1964, 158–159.

4. Portes and Rumbaut, 2001, 313.

5. See, for example, Gibson, 1989; Portes and Jensen, 1989; and Zhou, 1997

6. Gutierrez, 1995, 97.

7. Ibid.

8. Gutierrez, 1995, 78.

9. Marquez, 1993.

10. Garcia, 1997, 143.

11. Putnam, 2000.

12. See Montero, 1981; and Fugita and O'Brien, 1985.

13. See Collins, 1989; Durr and Logan, 1997; and Grodsky and Pager, 2001 for evidence that employee channeling on the basis of race marginalizes black professionals.

14. In response to the question, "How do you feel about current Affirmative Action policy?" 31 of the 50 interviewees said they were in favor of it, 16 were unsure or expressed a mixed opinion on the topic, one was opposed, and two had no opinion.

Chapter 4

1. See Choldin, 1986, 403–417; Rodriguez, 2000, 159; Espiritu, 1992, 112–133.

2. Hollinger, 1995, 19–50.

3. Edmonston and Passel, 1999, 407.

4. Harrison and Bennett, 1995, 166–167.

5. Qian, 1997, 267.

6. See Gurak and Fitzpatrick, 1982; Murguia, 1982; Qian, 1997; and Qian and Lichter, 2001.

7. Rumbaut, 1994.

8. My calculations derived from the 2002 Current Population Survey.

9. The Mexican-origin populations of New York City, Minneapolis, MN, Little Rock, AR, and Charlotte, NC, increased by approximately 200, 360, 400, and 1,200

percent, respectively, between 1990 and 2000 (Inter-University Program for Latino Research, 2005).

10. See Del Pinal and Singer, 1997, 31; and McKinnon and Humes, 2000), 2. Del Pinal and Singer found that 21 percent of Mexican-origin family households were headed by a single female, while McKinnon and Humes found this figure to be 45 percent among blacks.

11. Qian, 1997, 266.

12. Alba, 1985; and Perlmann, 1998.

13. Gordon, 1964, 80.

14. Alba, 1990, 12. See also, Lieberson and Waters, 1988.

15. Massey, 1995; Qian and Lichter, 2001.

16. Alba, 1990, 12.

17. This finding is consistent with that of Rosenfeld, 2002, based on 1990 census data.

18. For third-generation "unmixed Italian" husbands and wives, Alba (1985, 146) found rates of marriage with people of no Italian ancestry to be 67.3 and 62.1 percent, respectively, using data from the 1979 Current Population Survey.

19. Cazares, Murguia, and Frisbie, 1984; Hwang, Saenz, and Aguirre, 1995; Murguia and Frisbie, 1977; Sandefur and Mckinnel, 1986; Schoen, Nelson, and Collins, 1978; Schoen and Cohen, 1980.

20. Gordon, 1964, 69.

21. Alba and Nee, 1997.

22. Gordon, 1964, 159.

23. Granovetter, 1973, 201.

24. Lieberson and Waters, 1988.

25. Cready and Saenz, 1997; Mittelbach and Moore, 1968; Schoen and Cohen, 1980.

26. Anderson and Saenz, 1994, 418; Blau, Blum, and Schwartz, 1982; Blau and Schwartz, 1984; Fitzpatrick and Hwang, 1992.

27. Massey, 1995.

28. Lieberson, 1981, 380.

29. Blau, 1977; Blau and Schwartz, 1984; Hwang, Saenz, and Aguirre, 1997.

30. Anderson and Saenz, 1994, 417.

31. Cready and Saenz, 1997; Hwang, Saenz, and Aguirre, 1997; Qian, 1999.

32. Bean and Bradshaw, 1970; Cazares, Murguia, and Frisbie, 1984; Murguia and Frisbie, 1977; Schoen, Nelson, and Collins, 1978; Cready and Saenz, 1997.

33. Figure 4.1 employs the following conversion calculation of estimated logit coefficients in Model 2 of table 4.9 to predicted probabilities:

$Pr(y = 1) = exp(x'b) / [1 + exp(x'b)],$

where $Pr(y = 1)$ is the probability that a person is intermarried to an Anglo, x is a vector of the explanatory variables, and b is the estimated logit coefficients of the explanatory variables. Unless otherwise specified, panels A, B, and C in figure 4.1 hold constant other variables in the model such that the hypothetical Mexican American spouse in question has attained a high school diploma, is at least three generations from immigration, and lives in the Southwest region in an MSA where structural variables are held at the sample mean.

34. England and Farkas, 1986; Lichter et al., 1992; South, 1991, 92; Chiswick and Sullivan, 1995.

35. A model not shown here that included an interaction variable between generation and percent foreign-born failed to demonstrate that the magnitude of this effect varied by the immigrant generation of the respondent.

36. Larger cell sizes for interactions would be preferable for additional confirmation, but there is suggestive evidence here that the negative effect of status diversity on Mexican-origin/Anglo intermarriage found in Model 2 applies primarily to the first generation. If this is the case, where there is greater status diversity among the Mexican-origin population as a whole, there is also likely a concentration of the first generation in the lower strata whose likelihood of intermarriage is more strongly affected by its generational status than it would be within a less socio-economically stratified Mexican-origin subpopulation.

37. Massey, 1995, 640–643.

38. Bean et al., 2001, 26.

Chapter 5

1. Alba, 1985.

2. Waters, 1990.

3. See Tuan, 1998 for an exception to this tendency.

4. Alba, 1990, 318.

5. Portes and Zhou, 1993; and Zhou, 1997.

6. Portes and Zhou (1993) also propose a third adaptation to the new opportunity structure of assimilation that involves a strategy of deliberately preserving an immigrant community's values and solidarity to protect younger generations from the negative aspects of American popular culture and hence improve the chances of cross-generational economic advancement. This particular route applies mainly to immigrant enclaves and subgroups that have been able to selectively utilize cultural traits and ethnic institutions that have proven adaptive to their new environment; it has not been shown to be a dominant strategy among the Mexican-origin population.

7. Alba and Nee, 1997, 848.

8. Lieberson, 1981, 380.

9. Waters, 1990, 166.

10. Omi and Winant, 1994, 60.

11. Omi and Winant, 1994, 71.

12. Omi and Winant, 1994, 90.

13. See also Almaguer, 1992

14. See also Alba, 1990; and Gans, 1979.

15. See Espiritu, 1992; Nagel, 1996; and Jenkins, 1997.

16. Cornell and Hartmann, 1998, 83.

17. Cornell and Hartmann, 1998, 77.

18. See Oboler, 1995.

19. Garcia, 1997, 143.

20. Saenz and Aguirre, 1991, 27.

21. Though there is some truth to the claim that many New Mexican Hispanos are direct descendants of the Spanish conquistadors who wrested the territory from native pueblos some 400 years ago, recent historical research points to the early modern period beginning at the end of the nineteenth century as the time when Spanish American nomenclature came into prominence. Native Hispanos wielded Spanish ethnicity strategically as part of their effort to lay claim to their New Mexican homeland in the face of mounting Anglo regional dominance. Before then, in the spirit of Mexican independence, Spanish identification was rarely used. See Gonzales, 1997, 124–25.

22. Steinberg, 2001, 77–80.

23. Gutierrez, 1995, 195–99.

24. See Menchaca, 1995; Ochoa, 2004; and Pardo, 1998.

25. Saenz and Aguirre, 1991, 27.

26. See Almaguer, 1992; and Barrera, 1979.

27. See Espino and Franz, 2002; Murguia and Telles, 1990; Murguia and Telles, 1996.

28. Ignatiev, 1995; Jacobson, 1998; and Roediger, 1999.

29. Lieberson, 1981, 380. Using 1980 census data from 53 metropolitan statistical areas in the Southwest, Anderson and Saenz (1994, 421) find that relative group size of the Mexican-origin population has a statistically significant negative effect on the rate of Anglo/Mexican-origin intermarriage in the Mexican-origin population in a multivariate regression model that takes into account Anglo/Mexican-origin status inequality in education, internal Mexican-origin status diversity, Spanish language maintenance, log group size, sex ratio, and percent foreign-born in the Mexican-origin population.

Chapter 6

1. Babbie, 1995, 93.
2. Mills, 1959, 3–24.
3. Rodriguez, 2002, 10–11.
4. Davila, 2001, 69.
5. Klor de Alva, 1996, 59.
6. Ibid.
7. Cope, 1994, 162–165.
8. Chance, 1979, 160.
9. Chance, 1979, 164–165.
10. Vasconcelos, 1997.
11. Klor de Alva, 1996, 66; and Martinez-Echazabal, 1998, 37–38.
12. McAdam, 1982.
13. Omi and Winant, 1994, 87.
14. In the late sixties, Raza Unida leaders traveled to the South on various occasions to meet with Carmichael and other Civil Rights activists to learn how to organize and recruit for their own incipient movement. See Garcia, 1989, 16–17.
15. Chance, 1979, 160.
16. Gonzales, 1999, 115–117.
17. Griswold del Castillo and de Leon, 1997, 87.
18. Smith and Edmonston, 1997, 29; Reimers, 1998, 141; Schaefer, 1998, 113; and Sierra et al., 2000, 536.
19. In this regard, it is notable that anti-immigrant fervor reached its height in the mid-1990s at the end of an extended economic recession and then all but disappeared from the public's consciousness during the economic boom of the second half of the decade. Given the extended economic slowdown at the beginning of the present decade, this time during a period of heightened concern for national security, one might suspect it is only a matter of time before anti-immigrant sentiment once again becomes a central political theme, especially in those parts of the country receiving the highest volume of immigration.
20. See Jaynes and Williams, 1989, 7; and Waters and Eschbach, 1995, 431.
21. Griswold del Castillo and de Leon, 1997, 110–113.
22. See Garcia, 1997, Ch. 6, for a discussion of the institutionalization and mainstreaming of Chicano politics.
23. Hollinger, 1995, 19–50.
24. Rodriguez, 2000, 153–163; Root, 1992, 342–347; and Root, 2001, 160.
25. Rodriguez, 2000, 170–172.
26. Anzaldúa, 1987. See also, Alvarez, 1995; Bonilla et al., 1998; Flores, 1993;

Lugo, 2000; Maciel and Herrera-Sobek, 1998; Michaelsen and Johnson, 1997; Oboler, 1995; and Velez-Ibáñez, 1996.

27. Almaguer, 1992; Anderson and Saenz, 1994; Barrera, 1979; Bean and Tienda, 1987; Bean et al., 2001; Massey et al., 1987; Murguia, 1982; Portes and Rumbaut, 2001; and Saenz and Aguirre, 1991.

28. De la Garza et al., 1992, 12; and Harwood, 2002.

29. Cooper, 2005.

30. Wingett, 2004.

31. Kurtzman, 2005.

Bibliography

Adams, Jan. 1995. "Proposition 187 Lessons." *Z Magazine*, March.
< http://www.zmag.org/zmag/articles/mar95adams.htm> (1 July 2005).

Alba, Richard. 1985. *Italian Americans: Into the Twilight of Ethnicity*. Englewood Cliffs, NJ: Prentice Hall, Inc.

———. 1990. *Ethnic Identity: The Transformation of White America*. New Haven: Yale University Press.

Alba, Richard, John R. Logan, Brian J. Stults, Gilbert Marzan, and Wenquan Zhang. 1999. "Immigration Groups in the Suburbs: A Reexamination of Suburbanization and Spatial Assimilation." *American Sociological Review* 64:446–460.

Alba, Richard, and Victor Nee. 1997. "Rethinking Assimilation Theory for a New Era of Immigration." *International Migration Review* 31:826–874.

Almaguer, Tomás. 1992. *Racial Fault Lines: The Historical Origins of White Supremacy in California*. Berkeley: University of California Press.

Alvarez, Robert R. Jr. 1995. "The Mexican–U.S. Border: The Making of an Anthropology of Borderlands." *Annual Review of Anthropology* 24:447–470.

Anderson, Benedict. 1983. *Imagined Communities: Reflections on the Origin and Spread of Nationalism*. London: Verso.

Anderson, Robert N., and Rogelio Saenz. 1994. "Structural Determinants of Mexican American Intermarriage, 1975–1980." *Social Science Quarterly* 75:414–430.

Anzaldúa, Gloria. 1987. *Borderlands/La Frontera: The New Mestiza*. San Francisco: Spinsters/Aunt Lute.

Babbie, Earl. 1995. *The Practice of Social Research*. Belmont, CA: Wadsworth Publishing.

Bankston, Carl L., and Jacques Henry. 1999. "Endogamy among Louisiana Cajuns: A Social Class Explanation." *Social Forces* 77:1317–1338.

Barrera, Mario. 1979. *Race and Class in the Southwest: A Theory of Racial Inequality*. Notre Dame: University of Notre Dame Press.

Bean, Frank, and Stephanie Bell-Rose. 1999. *Immigration and Opportunity: Race, Ethnicity, and Employment in the United States*. New York: Russell Sage.

Bean, Frank D., and Benjamin S. Bradshaw. 1970. "Intermarriage between Persons of Spanish and Non-Spanish Surname: Changes from the Mid-19th to the Mid-20th Century." *Social Science Quarterly* 51:389–395.

Bean, Frank D., and Martha Tienda. 1987. *The Hispanic Population of the United States*. New York: Russell Sage Foundation.

Bean, Frank D., Stephen J. Trejo, Randy Capps, and Michael Tyler. 2001. *The Latino Middle Class: Myth, Reality, and Potential*. Claremont, CA: Tomas Rivera Policy Institute.

Billeaud, Jacques. 2004. "Prop. 200 Won Support from Blue-collar Workers." From *The Associated Press*, November 3. <http://www.azcentral.com/specials/special29/articles/1103200exit03-ON.html> (1 July 2005).

Blau, Peter. 1977. *Inequality and Heterogeneity*. New York: Free Press.

Blau, Peter M., Terry C. Blum, and Joseph E. Schwartz. 1982. "Heterogeneity and Intermarriage." *American Sociological Review* 47:45–62.

Blau, Peter M., and Joseph E. Schwartz. 1984. *Crosscutting Social Circles: Testing a Macro-structural Theory of Intergroup Relations*. New York: Academic Press.

Blauner, Robert. 1979. *Racial Oppression in America*. New York: Harper and Row.

Bonilla, Frank, Edwin Melendez, Rebecca Morales, and Maria de los Angeles Torres. 1998. *Borderless Borders: U.S. Latinos, Latin Americans, and the Paradox of Interdependence*. Philadelphia: Temple University Press.

Cazares, Ralph B., Edward Murguia, and W. Parker Frisbie. 1984. "Mexican American Intermarriage in a Nonmetropolitan Context." *Social Science Quarterly* 65:626–634.

Chance, John K. 1979. "Research Reports and Notes: On the Mexican Mestizo." *Latin American Research Review* 14:153–168.

Chavez, Leo R. 1994. "The Power of the Imagined Community: The Settlement of Undocumented Mexicans and Central Americans in the United States." *American Anthropologist* 96:52–73.

Chiswick, Barry R., and Teresa A. Sullivan. 1995. "The New Immigrants." Pp. 211–270 in *State of the Union: America in the 1990s*, edited by R. Farley. New York: Russell Sage.

Choldin, Harvey. 1986. "Statistics and Politics: The 'Hispanic Issue' in the 1980 Census." *Demography* 23:403–417.

Collins, Sharon. 1989. "The Marginalization of Black Executives." *Social Problems* 36:317–331.

Consejo Nacional de Población. 2001. "Migrantes mexicanos en los Estados Unidos." *Migración Internacional* 15:1–4.

Cooper, Marc. 2005. "High Noon on the Border." *The Nation*, June 6. <http://www.thenation.com/doc.mhtml%3Fi=20050606&s=cooper> (1 July 2005).

Cope, R. Douglas. 1994. *The Limits of Racial Domination: Plebian Society in Colonial Mexico, 1660–1720*. Madison: University of Wisconsin Press.

Cornell, Stephen, and Douglas Hartmann. 1998. *Ethnicity and Race: Making Identities in a Changing World*. Thousand Oaks, CA: Pine Forge Press.

Cready, Cynthia M., and Rogelio Saenz. 1997. "The Nonmetro/metro Context of Racial/ethnic Outmarriage: Some Differences between African Americans and Mexican Americans." *Rural Sociology* 62:335–362.

Davila, Arlene. 2001. *Latinos, Inc.: The Marketing and Making of a People*. Berkeley: University of California.

De la Garza, Rodolfo O., Louis DeSipio, F. Chris Garcia, and John Garcia. 1992. *Latino Voices: Mexican, Puerto Rican, and Cuban Perspectives on American Politics*. San Francisco: Westview Press.

Del Pinal, Jorge, and Audrey Singer. 1997. "Generations of Diversity: Latinos in the United States." *Population Bulletin* 52:1–31.

Dimas, Peter R. 1999. *Progress and a Mexican American Community's Struggle for Existence: Phoenix's Golden Gate Barrio*. New York: Peter Lang Publishing.

Donner, Henriette. 2001. "Under the Cross—Why V.A.D.s Performed the Filthiest Tasks in the Dirtiest War: Red Cross Women Volunteers, 1914–1918." *Journal of Social History* 30:687–704.

Durr, Marlese, and John R. Logan. 1997. "Racial Submarkets in Government: African American Managers in New York State." *Sociological Forum* 12:353–370.

Edmonston, Barry, and Jeffrey Passel. 1999. "How Immigration and Intermarriage Affect the Racial and Ethnic Composition of the U.S. Population." Pp. 373–414 in *Immigration and Opportunity: Race, Ethnicity, and Employment in the United States*, edited by F. Bean and S. B. Rose. New York: Russell Sage Foundation.

England, Paula, and George Farkas. 1986. *Households, Employment, and Gender: A Social Economic, and Demographic View*. New York: Aldine.

Espino, Rodolfo, and Michael Franz. 2002. "Latino Phenotypic Discrimination Revisited: The Impact of Skin Color on Occupational Status." *Social Science Quarterly* 83:612–623.

Espiritu, Yen Le. 1992. *Asian American Panethnicity: Bridging Institutions and Identities*. Philadelphia: Temple University Press.

Farley, Reynolds. 1995. "State of the Union: America in the 1990s, Volume Two: Social Trends." New York: Russell Sage.

———. 1995. "State of the Union: America in the 1990s." New York: Russell Sage Foundation.

Fitzpatrick, Kevin M., and Sean-Shong Hwang. 1992. "The Effects of Community Structure on Opportunities for Interracial Contact: Extending Blau's Macrostructural Theory." *Sociological Quarterly* 33:51–61.

Flores, Juan. 1993. *Divided Borders: Essays on Puerto Rican Identity*. Houston: Arte Publico Press.

Fox, Geoffrey. 1996. *Hispanic Nation: Culture, Politics, and the Construction of Identity*. Tucson: University of Arizona Press.

Fugita, Stephen, and David J. O'Brien. 1985. "Structural Assimilation, Ethnic Group Membership, and Political Participation among Japanese Americans: A Research Note." *Social Forces* 63:986–995.

Gans, Herbert J. 1979. "Symbolic Ethnicity: The Future of Ethnic Groups and Cultures in America." *Racial and Ethnic Studies* 2:1–20.

Garcia, Ignacio M. 1989. *United We Win: The Rise and Fall of La Raza Unida Party*. Tucson: Mexican American Studies and Resource Center, University of Arizona.

————. 1997. *Chicanismo: The Forging of a Militant Ethnos among Mexican Americans*. Tucson: University of Arizona Press.

Gibbs, Jack P., and Dudley L. Poston Jr. 1975. "The Division of Labor: Conceptualization and Related Measures," *Social Forces* 53:468–476.

Gibson, Margaret A. 1989. *Accommodation Without Assimilation: Sikh Immigrants in an American High School*. Ithaca: Cornell University Press.

Giddens, Anthony. 1991. *Modernity and Self-identity: Self and Society in the Late Modern Age*. Cambridge, U.K.: Polity Press.

Gonzales, Manuel. 1999. *Mexicanos: A History of Mexican Americans in the United States*. Bloomington: Indiana University Press.

Gonzales, Phillip B. 1997. "The Categorical Meaning of Spanish American Identity among Blue-collar New Mexicans, circa 1983." *Hispanic Journal of Behavioral Sciences* 19:123–136.

Gordon, Milton. 1964. *Assimilation in American Life: The Role of Race, Religion, and National Origins*. New York: Oxford University Press.

Granovetter, Mark S. 1973. "The Strength of Weak Ties." *American Journal of Sociology* 78:201–233.

Griswold del Castillo, Richard, and Arnoldo de Leon. 1997. *North to Aztlan: A History of Mexican Americans in the United States*. New York: Twayne.

Grodsky, Eric, and Devah Pager. 2001. "The Structure of Disadvantage: Individual and Occupational Determinants of the Black-White Wage Gap." *American Sociological Review* 66:542–567.

Gurak, Douglas T., and Joseph Fitzpatrick. 1982. "Intermarriage among Hispanic Ethnic Groups in New York City." *American Journal of Sociology* 87:921–934.

Gutierrez, David. 1995. *Walls and Mirrors: Mexican Americans, Mexican Immigrants, and the Politics of Ethnicity*. Berkeley: University of California Press.

Hackenberg, Robert A., and Nick Benequista. 2001. "The Future of an Imagined Community: Trailer Parks, Tree Huggers, and Trinational Forces Collide in the Southern Arizona Borderlands." *Human Organization* 60:153–158.

Harrison, Roderick J., and Claudette E. Bennett. 1995. "Racial and Ethnic Diversity." Pp. 141–210 in *State of the Union: America in the 1990s*, edited by R. Farley. New York: Russell Sage.

Harwood, John. 2002. "Bush Outreach to Hispanics Pays Dividends—Poll Shows a Major Gain with Crucial Group, But GOP Candidates Haven't Benefited." *The Wall Street Journal*, May 21. <http://www.wrnha.org/Issues%20News%20Articles/Polls%20and%20Surveys/Bush%20Outreach%20to%20Hispanics%20Pays%20Dividends%20for%20President.htm> (1 July 2005).

Hollinger, David. 1995. *Postethnic America*. New York: Basic Books.

Hwang, Sean-Shong, Rogelio Saenz, and Benigno E. Aguirre. 1995. "The SES Selectivity of Interracially Married Asians." *International Migration Review* 29:469–491.

————. 1997. "Structural Assimilationist Explanations of Asian American Intermarriage." *Journal of Marriage and the Family* 59:758–772.

Ignatiev, Noel. 1995. *How the Irish Became White*. New York: Routledge.

Inter-University Program for Latino Research. 2005. "Population Change for Mexican by Place" <http://www3.nd.edu/~iuplr/cicdata.php?Level1=6&Level2=2&go=Go> (5 July 2005).

Jacobs, Ronald N. 2002. "Civil Society and Crisis: Culture, Discourse, and the Rodney King Beating." *American Journal of Sociology* 101:1238–1272.

Jacobson, Matthew Frye. 1998. *Whiteness of a Different Color*. Cambridge: Harvard University Press.

Jaynes, Gerald David, and Robin M. Williams Jr., eds. 1989. *A Common Destiny: Blacks and American Society*. Washington, DC: National Academy Press.

———. 1989. "Summary and Conclusions." Pp. 1–25 in *A Common Destiny: Blacks and American Society*, edited by G. D. Jaynes and Robin M. Williams Jr. Washington, DC: National Academy Press.

Jenkins, Richard. 1997. *Rethinking Ethnicity: Arguments and Explorations*. Thousand Oaks, CA: Sage.

Katzew, Ilona, Elena I. Estrada De Gerlero, and Maria C. Garcia Saiz. 1996. *New World Orders: Casta Paintings and Colonial Latin America*. New York: Americas Society Art Gallery.

Klor de Alva, J. Jorge. 1996. "Mestizaje from New Spain to Aztlan: On the Control and Classification of Collective Identities." Pp. 42–71 in *New World Orders: Casta Paintings and Colonial Latin America*, edited by I. Katzew et al. New York: Americas Society Art Gallery.

Kurtzman, Laura. 2005. "Mayoral Landslide: L.A. Picks Villaraigosa." *The San Jose Mercury News*, May 18. <http://www.mercurynews.com/mld/mercurynews/11674551.htm> (1 July 2005).

Lichter, Daniel, Diane K. McLaughlin, George Kephart, and David J. Landry. 1992. "Race and the Retreat from Marriage: A Shortage of Marriageable Men?" *American Sociological Review* 57:781–799.

Lieberson, Stanley. 1981. *A Piece of the Pie: Blacks and White Immigrants since 1880*. Berkeley: University of California Press.

Lieberson, Stanley, and Mary C. Waters. 1988. *From Many Strands: Racial and Ethnic Groups in Contemporary America*. New York: Russell Sage.

Luckingham, Bradford. 1994. *Minorities in Phoenix: A Profile of Mexican American, Chinese American, and African American Communities, 1860–1992*. Tucson: University of Arizona Press.

Lugo, Alejandro. 2000. "Theorizing Border Inspections." *Cultural Dynamics* 12:353–373.

Maciel, David R., and Maria Herrera-Sobek. 1998. *Culture Across Borders: Mexican Immigration and Popular Culture*. Tucson: University of Arizona Press.

Malkki, Liisa H. 1995. *Purity and Exile: Violence, Memory, and National Cosmology among Hutu Refugees in Tanzania*. Chicago: University of Chicago Press.

Marquez, Benjamin. 1993. *LULAC: The Evolution of a Mexican American Political Organization*. Austin: University of Texas.

Martinez-Echazabal, Lourdes. 1998. "Mestizaje and the Discourse of National/Cultural Identity in Latin America." *Latin American Perspectives* 25:21–42.

Massey, Douglas S. 1985. "Ethnic Residential Segregation: A Theoretical Synthesis and Empirical Review." *Sociology and Social Research* 69:315–350.

———. 1995. "The New Immigration and Ethnicity in the United States." *Population and Development Review* 21:631–652.

Massey, Douglas S., and Nancy A. Denton. 1992. "Racial Identity and the Spatial Assimilation of Mexicans in the United States." *Social Science Quarterly* 21:235–260.

Massey, Douglas S. et al. 1987. *Return to Aztlan: The Social Process of Immigration from Western Mexico*. Berkeley: University of California Press.

McAdam, Doug. 1982. *The Political Process and the Development of Black Insurgency*. Chicago: University of Chicago Press.

McKinnon, Jesse, and Karen Humes. 2000. *The Black Population of the United States: March 1999*. Washington, DC: U.S. Census Bureau.

Menchaca, Martha. 1995. *The Mexican Outsiders: A Community History of Marginalization and Discrimination in California*. Austin: University of Texas.

Michaelson, Scott, and David E. Johnson. 1997. *Border Theory: The Limits of Cultural Politics*. Minneapolis: University of Minnesota Press.

Mills, C. Wright. 1959. *The Sociological Imagination*. New York: Grove Press.

Mittelbach, Frank G., and Joan W. Moore. 1968. "Ethnic Endogamy—The Case of Mexican Americans." *American Journal of Sociology* 74:50–62.

Montero, Darrel. 1981. "The Japanese Americans: Changing Patterns of Assimilation over Three Generations." *American Sociological Review* 46:829–839.

Murguia, Edward. 1982. *Chicano Intermarriage: A Theoretical and Empirical Study*. San Antonio, TX: Trinity University Press.

Murguia, Edward, and W. Parker Frisbie. 1977. "Trends in Mexican American Intermarriage: Recent Findings in Perspective." *Social Science Quarterly* 58:374–389.

Murguia, Edward, and Edward Telles. 1990. "Phenotypic Discrimination and Income Differences among Mexican Americans." *Social Science Quarterly* 71:682–696.

———. 1996. "Phenotype and Schooling among Mexican Americans." *Sociology of Education* 69:276–89.

Nagel, Joane. 1996. *American Indian Ethnic Renewal: Red Power and the Resurgence of Identity and Culture*. New York: Oxford University Press.

Neidert, Lisa, and Reynolds Farley. 1985. "Assimilation in the United States: An Analysis of Ethnic and Generation Differences in Status and Achievement." *American Sociological Review* 50:840–850.

Oboler, Suzanne. 1995. *Ethnic Labels, Latino Lives: Identity and the Politics of (Re)Presentation in the United States*. Minneapolis: University of Minnesota Press.

Ochoa, Gilda. 2004. *Becoming Neighbors in a Mexican American Community: Power Conflict and Solidarity.* Austin: University of Texas Press.

Olmos, Edward James, Lea Ybarra, and Manuel Monterrey. 1999. *Americanos: Latino Life in the United States.* Boston: Little, Brown and Company.

Omi, Michael, and Howard Winant. 1994. *Racial Formation in the United States: From the 1960s to the 1990s.* New York: Routledge.

Pardo, Mary S. 1998. *Mexican American Women Activists: Identity and Resistance in Two Los Angeles Communities.* Philadelphia: Temple University Press.

Perlmann, Joel. 1998. "The Romance of Assimilation? Studying the Demographic Outcomes of Ethnic Intermarriage in American History." Working Paper No. 230, The Levy Economics Institute of Bard College.

Perlmann, Joel, and Roger Waldinger. 1997. "Second Generation Decline? Children of Immigrations, Past and Present—A Reconsideration." *International Migration Review* 31:893–922.

Pitti, Stephen J. 2003. *The Devil in Silicon Valley: Northern California, Race, and Mexican Americans.* Princeton: Princeton University Press.

Portes, Alejandro, and Leif Jensen. 1989. "The Enclave and the Entrants: Patterns of Ethnic Enterprise in Miami before and after Mariel." *American Sociological Review* 54:929–949.

Portes, Alejandro, and Ruben Rumbaut. 2001. "Conclusion—Forging of a New America: Lessons for Theory and Policy." Pp. 301–318 in *Ethnicities: Children of Immigrants in America,* edited by A. Portes and R. Rumbaut. Berkeley: University of California Press.

———. 2001. *Ethnicities: Children of Immigrants in America.* Berkeley: University of California Press.

Portes, Alejandro, and Min Zhou. 1993. "The New Second Generation: Segmented Assimilation and its Variants among Post-1965 Immigrant Youth." *Annals of the American Academy of Political and Social Science* 530:74–98.

Putnam, Robert. 2000. *Bowling Alone: The Collapse and Revival of American Community.* New York: Simon and Schuster.

Qian, Zhenchao. 1997. "Breaking the Racial Barriers: Variations in Interracial Marriage between 1980 and 1990." *Demography* 34:263–276.

———. 1999. "Who Intermarries? Education, Nativity, Region, and Interracial Marriage, 1980 and 1990." *Journal of Comparative Family Studies* 30:579–597.

Qian, Zhenchao, and Daniel T. Lichter. 2001. "Measuring Marital Assimilation: Intermarriage among Natives and Immigrants." *Social Science Research* 30:289–312.

Reimers, David M. 1998. *Unwelcome Strangers: American Identity and the Turn Against Immigration.* New York: Columbia University Press.

Rodriguez, Clara E. 2000. *Changing Race: Latinos, the Census, and the History of Ethnicity in the United States.* New York: New York University Press.

Rodriguez, Joseph A. 1999. *City Against Suburb: The Cultural Wars in an American Metropolis.* Westport, CT: Praeger Publishing.

Rodriguez, Richard. 2002. *Brown: The Last Discovery of America*. New York: Viking.

Roediger, David R. 1999. *The Wages of Whiteness: Race and the Making of the American Working Class*. New York: Verso.

Rohrlich, Ted. 1997. "Latino Voting in California Surged in 1996 Election." *The Los Angeles Times*, December 31. <http://www.azteca.net/aztec/immigrat/politics2.html> (1 July 2005).

Root, Maria P. P. 1992. "From Shortcuts to Solutions." Pp. 342–347 in *Racially Mixed People in America*, edited by M.P.P. Root. Newbury Park, CA: Sage.

———. 1992. *Racially Mixed People in America*. Newbury Park, CA: Sage.

———. 2001. *Love's Revolution*. Philadelphia: Temple University Press.

Rosenfeld, Michael J. 2002. "Measures of Assimilation in the Marriage Market: Mexican Americans 1970–1990." *Journal of Marriage and Family* 64:152–162.

Rumbaut, Ruben. 1994. "The Crucible Within: Ethnic Identity, Self-esteem, and Segmented Assimilation among Children of Immigrants." *International Migration Review* 18:748–794.

———. 1997. "Assimilation and Its Discontents." *International Migration Review* 31:923–960.

Saenz, Rogelio, and Benigno Aguirre. 1991. "The Dynamics of Mexican Ethnic Identity." *Ethnic Groups* 9:17–32.

Sandefur, Gary, and Trudy Mckinnel. 1986. "American Indian Intermarriage." *Social Science Research* 15:347–371.

Schaefer, Richard T. 1998. *Racial and Ethnic Groups*. New York: Longman.

Schoen, Robert, and Lawrence E. Cohen. 1980. "Ethnic Endogamy among Mexican American Grooms: A Reanalysis of Generational and Occupational Effects." *American Journal of Sociology* 86:359–366.

Schoen, Robert, Verne E. Nelson, and Marion Collins. 1978. "Intermarriage among Spanish Surnamed Californians, 1962–1974." *International Migration Review* 12:259–269.

Shorris, Earl. 1992. *Latinos: A Biography of the People*. New York: W. W. Norton.

Sierra, Christine Marie, Teresa Carrillo, and Louis DeSipio. 2000. "Latino Immigration and Citizenship." *Political Science and Politics* 33:534–540.

Smith, James P., and Barry Edmonston. 1997. *The New Americans: Economic, Demographic, and Fiscal Effects of Immigration*. Washington, DC: National Academic Press.

South, Scott J. 1991. "Sociodemographic Differences in Mate Selection Preferences." *Journal of Marriage and the Family* 53:928–940.

Steinberg, Stephen. 2001. *The Ethnic Myth: Race, Ethnicity, and Class in America*. 3d ed. Boston: Beacon Press.

Suarez-Orozco, Marcelo M., and Mariela Paez. 2002. *Latinos: Remaking America*. Berkeley: University of California Press.

Suro, Robert. 1998. *Strangers Among Us: How Latino Immigration Is Transforming America*. New York: Alfred A. Knopf.

Telles, Edward, and Edward Murguia. 1996. "Phenotype and Schooling among Mexican Americans." *Sociology of Education* 69:276–289.

Tuan, Mia. 1998. *Forever Foreigners or Honorary Whites?* New Brunswick: Rutgers University Press.

Vasconcelos, Jose. 1997 (1924). *La Raza Cósmica: Misión de la Raza Iberoamericana.* Baltimore: Johns Hopkins University Press.

Velez-Ibáñez, Carlos G. 1996. *Border Visions: Mexican Cultures of the Southwest United States.* Tucson: University of Arizona Press.

Waters, Mary C. 1990. *Ethnic Options: Choosing Identities in America.* Berkeley: University of California Press.

Waters, Mary C., and Karl Eschbach. 1995. "Immigration and Ethnic and Racial Inequality in the United States." *Annual Review of Sociology* 21:419–446.

Wingett, Yvonne. 2004. "Younger Latinos React to Prop. 200: New Generation of Activist Born." *The Arizona Republic,* December 12. <http://www.azcentral.com/specials/special29/articles/1212Prop200-activist.html> (1 July 2005).

Wollenberg, Charles. 1985. *Golden Gate Metropolis: Perspectives on Bay Area History.* Berkeley, CA: Institute of Governmental Studies.

Zhou, Min. 1997. "Segmented Assimilation: Issues, Controversies, and Recent Research on the New Second Generation." *International Migration Review* 31:975–1008.

Index

acculturation, 22–23, 96; and
   intermarriage, 75, 79–80, 88, 91;
   selective, 46
activism: Chicano, 34, 44, 53, 122, 131;
   cross-generational, 22; minority
   group, 44; student, 20, 51
Affirmative Action policy, 9–10;
   attitudes towards, 151; and
   categorical ambiguity, 129; and
   Richard Rodriguez, 118; and
   structural assimilation, 23, 61–64
African Americans: and intermarriage,
   75, 77; market for, 61; and official
   categories of race, 127; and
   ongoing immigration, 92; and
   oppositional identity, 105; in
   Phoenix, 17; and social inequality,
   72–74; and social movements, 98–
   99, 103, 122; and white supremacy,
   114; and World War II, 122
African ancestry, 120
agriculture: and Mexican migration
   to the Southwest, 13–18; and
   occupational status, 72
Aguirre, Benigno, 105
Alba, Richard, 76, 95
Alianza Hispano-Americana, 19, 46–47
Almaguer, Tomás, 114
American Indians: and oppositional
   identity, 105; and white supremacy,
   114
American mainstream culture, 6, 65, 80

American Mestizaje, 13, 24, 44, 115,
   123, 132
American Southwest, 6, 44; and
   industrial agriculture, 15–16; and
   Mexican immigrant labor, 13, 92
Anderson, Benedict, 23, 26–27, 40–41
Anglo Americans, 9, 18; as coworkers,
   63, 65. See also whites
Anglo domination, 18, 34, 46, 154
Anglo-majority work environments, 16,
   54, 130
Anglo/Mexican-origin intermarriage,
   23, 68, 84, 90, 114, 154
Anglo settlers, 17
Anzaldúa, Gloria, 128
Arizona: and mining, 16; as part of
   Southwest region, 71, 78; and
   Proposition 200, 21, 126, 131–32
Arizona State Supreme Court, 17
Arizona State University, 20, 22, 51
Asian Americans, 7, 12, 149; and
   intermarriage, 75, 77
assigned identities, 106–10, 114–15
assimilation, 9, 18–20, 42, 60, 83, 93,
   126; classical, 24, 74; cultural,
   23, 59, 79, 80, 81, 84, 88, 91,
   124; identity, 22, 24, 96; and
   intermarriage, 75–76, 84, 88; and
   language loss, 34–35; measures
   of, 88; segmented, 9, 18, 19, 20, 45,
   96–99; structural, 22, 23, 58–59,
   61–65, 75, 80, 81, 91, 96; theory of,

79; and voluntary organizations, 45;
and the workplace, 55
Association of Latinos in Public
    Financing and Accounting, 59
Aztlán, 73, 79, 116

Barrera, Mario, 16
Black Power, 10
blacks. *See* African Americans
Blau, Peter, 81, 90
Bush, George W., 21, 128

California: and anti-immigrant politics,
    132; and ethnic enclaves, 45;
    and ongoing immigration, 115;
    and Proposition 187, 126; and
    Proposition 209, 62; as a regional
    category, 72–73, 84, 88; and the
    Southwest, 4, 17, 23, 53, 75, 78,
    130; and Spanish-language media,
    40; and the United Farm Workers
    Union, 112; and white supremacy,
    114
California Bar Association, 48, 58
canneries: in San Jose, 18
Carmichael, Stokeley, 122, 155
casta system, 120, 124
categorical ambiguity, 128–29
Catholic Church, 94
Catholicism, 29–30, 32, 102
Central America, 21, 76
Chance, John K., 120, 124
Chandler, Arizona, 4
Chávez, César, 20
Chicana identity, 34, 101–2, 103, 106, 107
Chicanismo, 105
Chicano ethos, 13, 47, 52–54, 57, 59, 65
Chicano identity, 20; and the Current
    Population Survey, 83; among
    third-plus generation, 94, 100–106,
    110, 111–13, 115
Chicano Movement, 9, 12, 20, 22, 34;
    and Chicano ethos, 52–53, 131;

and Chicano identity, 102; as
    cultural sellout, 35; and Mexican
    revolutionary iconography, 122,
    126; symbolic impact of, 47; and
    transformation of racial and ethnic
    identity, 44
Chicanos por la Causa, 20, 52, 53, 130
childcare, 21
children: English-speaking, 35–36;
    ethnic identity of, 68–69; and ethnic
    work, 61; of immigrants, 15, 70, 80,
    97, 117; middle-class, 116
Chinese Americans, 17, 18, 129, 149
citizenship: and Mexican American
    voluntary associations, 47; and
    Mexican immigration, 7
civic engagement, 48
civil rights legislation, 68, 99, 127
Civil Rights Movement: influence
    on Mexican American voluntary
    associations, 19–20, 126; and
    political opportunity, 121–22;
    symbolic impact of, 9, 12, 44
college education: and cultural
    knowledge, 108, 111; and ethnic
    work, 61; among Mexican
    Americans, 12, 105, 131; and
    volunteer work, 50–51
Colorado, 71, 78, 108
Congress, U.S., 125
Cope, Douglas R., 120
Cornell, Stephen, 99
cotton economy, 122
cotton farmers in Arizona, 15, 122
creole status, 120–21, 124–25
cross-national encounters, 38
Cuban Americans: and intermarriage,
    76–77; and Latino identity, 5; in
    Miami, Florida, 45; and official
    categories of race and ethnicity,
    127; political views of, 128
cultural assimilation, 23, 75, 79–81,
    84, 88

cultural dominance, 4, 23
cultural institutions, 9, 23, 25, 41
cultural knowledge, 41–42, 108, 119
cultural resources, 27, 32, 35, 40–41
culture, 18, 34; colonial, 27; corporate, 56–58; disembedded, 9; ethnic, 9, 39, 42, 67; mainstream, 130; mediated, 23, 41; Mexican, 27, 36, 38, 100, 112, 121, 122; pop, 45; regional, 83
Current Population Survey, 10, 69, 70, 76, 77, 83, 84

Dávila, Arlene, 119, 125
deindustrialization, 10
De la Garza, Rodolfo, et al., 128
Del Monte canneries, 18
Department of Labor Statistics, 10
desegregation, 10
Diaz, Porfirio, 14, 125
discrimination: and acculturation, 79; in job market, 74; language-based, 36; against Mexican Americans, 4, 17, 19; against minority groups, 68; and ongoing immigration, 97–98; reverse, 10, 63, 131; and voluntary organizations, 46
diversity: ethnic and racial, 56, 68; group status, 82, 91; language, 26; Latino, 4, 5
dominant society, 8, 10, 11, 41, 45, 122
dual wage system, 14

East San Jose, 20, 21, 94
Edmonston, Barry, 68
education, 4, 68, 82; bilingual, 118, 122, 129, 132; and economic mobility, 97; and first generation, 54; and phenotype, 114; public, 15, 61; social segregation of workers by, 57; and status inequality, 86; and voluntary associations, 51–53
educational attainment, 10, 72–75;

and attitudes toward language, 41; and ethnic identity, 95, 111; and intermarriage, 79–81, 91–93; and social class, 12; and social inequality, 126, 129–30; and social integration, 125, 131; and structural assimilation, 23, 88
endogamy, 75
ESL classes, 60
"ethclass," 80
ethnic community, 9–10, 15, 19, 27, 80, 93, 98, 117
ethnic concentration, 7–10, 24; and intermarriage, 88, 92, 93; and Mexican ethnicity, 114, 116, 129; and volunteer work, 54
ethnic consciousness, 47, 64, 65, 67, 93
ethnic enclave, 8, 45
ethnic food, 29–32, 41, 42
ethnic groups: as imagined communities, 26; intermarriage of, 75, 76; social distance between, 10; social integration of, 22–23, 45, 81. See also specific ethnic groups
ethnic guilt, 32
ethnic identity, 6, 8, 24, 95, 96, 99, 100, 103; and intermarriage, 69; movements, 9, 12, 44, 53, 54, 98; organization, 101; politics of, 44; professional organizations involving, 23, 43, 46, 58, 59, 65; in workplace, 54, 64
ethnic institutions, 10, 46
ethnicity, 3, 5, 119, 132; meaningful context of, 25, 26; and media, 40, 41, 98; official categories of, 24, 68, 73, 77; optional, 12, 103, 110, 112; situational, 103; symbolic, 6, 26, 65, 96; voluntary, 99, 115
ethnic networks, 8, 44
ethnic organizations, 19, 51, 111
ethnic revivalism, 6, 101
ethnic stereotypes, 97

ethnic work, 56, 61
ethnographic research, 11, 117
European Americans, 6, 7, 76, 92, 93, 95, 99, 113
European identities, 95, 110, 111, 113, 114
European immigrants, 9, 13, 15, 103, 112

Fair Housing Act, 68, 99, 127
family, 49, 91, 93, 111; first-generation, 21; household, 74, 93; mixed-ethnic, 12; and religion, 42; and traditional gender roles, 32
farm labor, 16
fascism, 19, 122
federal legislation, 9, 64, 65, 97, 98
Federal Office of Management and Budget, 127
Fiesta de las Rosas, 19, 20
Filipino Americans, 110, 127
first-generation immigrants: and assimilation theory, 96, 97, 98; and Chicana/o identity, 101; definition of, 70; and ethnic concentrations, 54; and ethnic work, 61; interacting with third-plus generation, 102; and intermarriage, 78, 83, 88, 90, 92, 153; and metro growth, 21; and qualitative research, 117; as regional working class, 38; socioeconomic gains of, 72
foreign-born population, 12, 69, 70, 86, 90, 119
Fort McDowell, 17
Fourteenth Amendment, 17
Fresno State, 50

Garcia, Ignacio, 47, 53, 54
gender, 23, 26, 35, 36, 62, 84, 90, 129; and traditional relations, 31–32, 41
gente de razón, 18
G.I. Forum, 19, 46, 47, 126

Golden Gate neighborhood, 20–21
Gonzales, Manuel, 15
Gordon, Milton, 45, 46, 58, 59, 75, 79, 80, 91
grandparents, 33, 38, 39
Great Depression, 16, 125
Great Flood, 17
Great Migration, 17
Gutierrez, David, 46

Habitat for Humanity, 49
Hartmann, Douglas, 99
Hawaii, 72, 109, 110
high school, 12, 72, 84
Hispanic Business Students Association (HBSA), 51–52
Hispanic Chamber of Commerce, 48
Hispanic ethnicity, 77, 98, 100, 104, 127
Hispanic/Latino/Spanish category, 68
Hispanic population, 3, 5, 55, 83
Hollinger, David, 127
homesteaders, 15
host society, 45, 65
housing construction, 21
housing segregation, 5, 19
hybridization, 4, 44

identity: and assimilation, 22, 96; European-origin, 95; large-scale group, 26, 67; minority group, 44, 122; professional, 44, 58, 59. See also ethnic identity; ethnicity
illegal immigration, 4
Illegal Immigration Act, 125
imagined communities, 23, 26–27, 40–42
immigrants, 3, 4, 8, 10, 65, 103, 110, 112; descendants of, 45–46, 95–97, 108, 112, 130; as labor, 21; Latino, 94, 119; Mexican, 8, 15, 38, 81, 103, 104, 115; scapegoating of, 16, 125; and social mobility, 97
immigration, 7, 8, 10, 18, 21, 69, 129–

30; and anti-immigrant politics, 132, 155; ethnic identity, 112, 114; and intermarriage, 75, 79, 92; ongoing, 24, 38, 66, 76, 81, 90, 91, 115; post-1965 "new," 6
Immigration Act, 12
immigration law, 6, 79, 97
income, 4, 12, 19, 74, 82, 95, 114
Indian ancestry, 120
indios bárbaros, 18
industrial agriculture, 16
industrial growth, 13
inequality, 10, 65, 68, 74, 90–93, 118, 121; internal group, 46
integrating environments, 11, 12, 26, 42, 131
integration, social, 4, 5, 7, 9–10, 23, 93; and cultural resources, 27; and ethnic identity, 115; and ethnic identity organizations, 19, 47, 58; and inequality, 132; and intermarriage, 75, 80, 81, 82, 91, 92; Mexican-American, 11, 41, 117; and regional context, 72, 74; spatial, 12; and the workplace, 55, 64, 65
inter-group status inequality, 24
intermarriage, 6, 68, 70, 72, 117, 125, 153; data, 79, 86, 114; in eighteenth-century New Spain, 124; among European Americans, 95, 96; inter-ethnic, 11, 90; as measure of social distance, 75–78; regional differences of, 92; social structural explanations of, 81, 82, 131
intermixing: social and cultural, 3
Irish Americans, 114
Italian Americans, 28, 36, 79, 93, 95, 98, 152
Italian identity, 108, 109, 110, 113, 114

Japanese Americans, 59, 129, 149
Japanese Citizens League, 68
Jewish Americans, 93, 114

Jim Crow Laws, 98
job: blue-collar, 16; networks, 15; stable working-class, 7; unionized, 10

King, Martin Luther, Jr., 122
Klor de Alva, J. Jorge, 120

language, 4, 9, 45, 79; as cultural resource, 26, 29, 33–36, 41; deficiencies, 17; and discipline, 35; English, 12; loss, 23, 34, 41; skills, 80; Spanish, 23, 32, 33, 37, 39, 102, 119
Latin America: and categories of race, 27, 67–68, 120, 121; immigration from, 3, 6–7, 12
Latina/o Studies, 117
Latinidad, 119, 121, 128
Latinos, 3, 5, 7, 118; and community, 49, 50, 53, 54; culture of, 39, 40, 113; demographic aspects of, 4, 10, 61, 63, 68, 69, 71, 128; ethnic identity of, 40, 104; immigrant, 4, 21, 132; and intermarriage, 76–77; marketing for, 60, 119; and media representation, 39–40, 48, 125; non-Mexican origin, 4, 84; and official census categories, 127–29; and voluntary associations, 50–54, 68; as voters, 21
League of United Latin American Citizens (LULAC), 19, 46, 47, 59
Lieberson, Stanley, 97, 98, 114
Lithuanian ethnicity, 25
Los Angeles, 15, 84, 112, 132
Luckingham, Bradford, 17

Madero, Francisco, 14
mainstream society, 44, 46, 63, 64, 75, 79, 95, 98
mariachi music, 25, 40, 108
Marquez, Benjamin, 47
Mazatlán, 37

McAdam, Doug, 121
mediated experience, 27, 41, 42, 43
mentoring work, 46, 50, 52, 59
meritocracy, 62, 63
Mesa, Arizona, 28, 33, 60, 101, 102, 106
mestizaje, 3, 5, 6, 24, 67, 115; American
    context of, 13–22; and official
    categories of race and ethnicity,
    127–33; social history of, 119–26
mestizos, 1, 3, 4, 13, 22, 120–24
metropolitan statistical areas, 83, 88, 90
Mexican American community, 50, 76
Mexican American Community Service
    Agency (MACSA), 20
Mexican American Political
    Association (MAPA), 20, 47
Mexican Americans, 4, 5, 8, 10, 122,
    126, 131, 132; and categorical
    ambiguity, 128–30; demographic
    aspects of, 15, 69, 83, 90, 93; and
    ethnic identity, 9, 23, 41, 44, 100,
    103–15; and intermarriage, 10,
    77, 81, 84, 88, 91, 92, 93; middle-
    class, 19, 21, 26, 47, 53, 58, 65;
    representation of in popular
    culture, 118, 119; and social
    mobility, 19, 125; and Spanish
    language ability, 34; and traditional
    gender roles, 32; U.S.–born,
    46, 103, 112, 116; and voluntary
    organizations, 45–46; war-veteran,
    19; working-class, 18; younger
    generation, 20
Mexican American Student
    Organization (MASA), 20, 62
Mexican Heritage Corporation, 25
Mexicanidad, 129
Mexican Revolution, 14, 16, 53, 121,
    122, 125–26
Mexicano identity, 3, 83, 104
Mexican-origin population, 7, 8, 23,
    66; and Chicano identity, 105,
    107; concentration of, 88, 90; and

ethnographic research, 117; and
    intermarriage, 83, 86, 92, 93, 154;
    and mestizaje, 124, 125, 127, 132;
    and multiple generation data set,
    69–70; sense of obligation towards,
    53; and symbolic ethnicity, 111
Mexicans, 8, 11; immigration of, 13,
    90, 92, 93, 114; interactions with
    third-plus generation, 36–38; and
    Mexican American identity, 104,
    108–10
Mexico, 7; contemporary migration
    from, 24, 76, 92, 112; early
    twentieth-century migration from,
    13–16; and official categories of
    race, 120–21, 123–24; respondents
    travel in, 36–39, 108
Mexico City, 28, 120
Miami, Florida, 40, 45
micro/macro connection, 117, 133
Midwest, 15, 71, 72, 79
Mills, C. Wright, 118
mining, 13–15, 17, 18, 102, 120
minorities, 9, 58, 64, 65, 68, 93, 98, 124;
    native-born, 6, 96, 105, 111; racial,
    99; representation of, 23, 44, 53, 59,
    62, 63, 65, 125; status of, 9, 54, 99;
    students, 20; working-class, 56
minuteman militia, 131
Mothers of East Los Angeles, 112
movimiento, 47, 59, 122
Movimiento Estudiantil Chicano de
    Aztlán (MEChA), 51–52
mutual aid societies, 15

National Council on La Raza, 68
nationalism, 26, 47, 121, 126
national-level data, 8, 69, 79
National Society of Hispanic MBAs, 58
network theory, 23, 80
New Mexico, 72, 78, 108, 110, 154
New Spain, 24, 67, 120, 124
Northern Arizona University, 51

Oaxaca, Mexico, 120
occupations, 5, 6, 9, 12, 16, 57, 68, 114;
    and social integration, 57, 74, 82
Ohlone Indians, 18
Omi, Michael, 98, 99, 122
organizations, 43, 76; Mexican
    American participation in, 46,
    76, 111; professional, 10, 48, 65;
    student, 51–52, 101, 111; voluntary,
    23, 45, 48, 49, 65

Pacific Northwest, 75
pan-ethnic identity, 40
parallel institutions, 45–46
parents, 9, 11, 15, 62, 68, 70, 116; and
    Spanish-language skills, 30, 35–36
Parent Teacher Association, 48
Passel, Jeffrey, 68
phenotype: and socioeconomic status,
    114
Phoenix, 4, 8, 11, 51, 100, 104, 109;
    Chicano activism in, 20; as context
    for Mexican ethnicity, 26–27, 38,
    54, 60, 63, 93, 130; early history of,
    17; growth since 1965, 21
Phoenix Community College, 101
Polish Americans, 93
political conservatism: among Latinos,
    128–29
political power, 14, 18, 121, 124
political process: and mestizaje, 121–26
Portes, Alejandro, 46
poverty, 45, 54
prejudice, 8, 10, 93, 109, 111, 113;
    and assimilation, 79; and ongoing
    immigration, 97
primary relationships, 45
Proposition 187, 21, 126
Proposition 200, 21, 22, 126, 131, 132
Proposition 209, 62
Puerto Ricans, 5, 69, 76, 77, 127, 128
Puerto Vallarta, 36, 37, 38
Putnam, Robert, 48

Qian, Zhenchao, 68
qualitative research, 7

race, 3, 6, 9, 11, 24, 49; and Affirmative
    Action, 64, 119; and intermarriage,
    76, 77; and mestizaje in Americas,
    120–26; and Mexican American
    identity, 114; official categories
    of, 68, 127–29; and segmented
    assimilation, 96, 98; social
    construction of, 99; and white
    supremacy, 14
racism, 9, 63, 94, 98
railroads, 13, 15
Raza Cósmica, 121
Raza Unida Party, 53, 122, 155
relational resources, 30, 35
relative group size, 81, 154
religion, 18, 23, 26, 29, 31, 41, 45;
    organized, 30, 79
repatriation, 16
restaurants, 27, 28
reverse discrimination, 10, 63, 65
Rodriguez, Richard, 19, 118, 119
Russian ethnicity, 108

Saenz, Rogelio, 105
Salt River Valley, 17
San Antonio, Texas, 122
San Francisco, California, 18, 28, 34,
    56, 57, 58
San Jose, California, 8, 11, 15, 25, 36–
    38, 51, 53, 55; Chicano activism in,
    20; early history of, 18–19; ethnic
    concentration of, 93, 108; growth of
    since 1965, 21; as social context for
    Mexican ethnicity, 26, 48, 54, 55,
    108, 110, 132
scholarship programs, 59
Scottsdale, Arizona, 25, 34, 102, 103
second generation, 21, 45, 67, 69,
    100, 117, 118, 130; defined, 70;
    and intermarriage, 77, 78, 83;

and segmented assimilation, 97;
socioeconomic gains of, 72, 74
segmented assimilation. *See*
assimilation
segregation, 17, 19, 47, 67, 68, 198;
housing, 5
"separate-but-equal" policies, 47
separatism, 9, 46, 53
Sikhs, 45
Silicon Valley, 21, 25, 62, 104, 110
Sky Harbor International Airport
(Phoenix), 21
social capital, 48
social class, 17, 39, 40, 46, 49, 58, 60, 80
social comfort, 56
social constructionism, 24, 67, 98–99, 120
social context, 4, 24, 25, 34, 41, 53, 76, 92
social control, 35, 120
social distance, 8, 10, 69, 75, 81, 92, 111
social inequality, 4, 7, 10, 24; in Latin
America, 121, 124, 125; and Latina/o
identity, 128–30; and Mexican
immigration, 92; and social
structure, 116; in the United States,
126; in workplace, 56
social justice, 22, 51
social mobility, 13, 80, 98, 124
social structure, 67, 75, 81, 83, 88, 99,
116, 119
Society for Hispanic Professional
Engineers, 58, 130
socioeconomic status, 66, 67, 74, 81
sociological imagination, 25, 118
Sonora, Mexico, 17
South America, 76
Southwest, 4, 8, 9, 107, 116; borderland
and, 128; Chicano activism in,
20; desegregation in, 126; early
twentieth-century occupations in,
16, 17; housing segregation in,
19; ongoing immigration within,
92, 115; race ideology in, 114; as
a regional category, 71–73, 75, 78,

88; size of the Latino population in,
53, 60, 130; and social construction
of Mexican ethnicity, 44; and U.S.–
Mexican War, 14
Spain, 18, 36, 108, 120, 121
Spanish American identity, 110, 154
Spanish colonies, 18, 121
Spanish ethnicity, 83
Spanish language, 29, 32, 37, 39, 41, 102,
108, 119; ability, 30, 38–39, 103, 117;
and electronic media, 4, 26, 39–42;
and grandparents, 33; knowledge of,
40, 42, 116; and students, 60, 61
spatial integration, 12
Special Olympics, 48
spouses, 79, 92; non-Latino, 68
status diversity, 82, 91, 153, 154
status inequality, 24, 82, 86
Steinberg, Stephen, 112
stereotypes, 8, 10, 24; ethnic food and,
28; and media representation, 119;
and ongoing immigration, 97, 114;
in workplace, 62, 63, 131
stratification: economic, 82; ethnic, 92;
social, 10, 14
structural assimilation. *See* assimilation
structural pluralism, 45
suburban life, 8, 12, 20, 95
Sunbelt cities, 20, 21
Supreme Court, 47, 61
symbolic ethnicity, 6, 24, 27, 65, 111

television, 39, 40, 41, 42
Tempe, Arizona, 22
Texas: and Chicano activism, 102,
122; as regional category, 71, 72,
73, 75, 78, 84, 88; and voluntary
organizations, 47, 116
third generation, 6, 45, 77, 95, 96–97
third-plus generation, 6, 37, 69, 70,
72, 76, 78, 93; blacks, 74; ethnic
groups, 12; European Americans, 7,
39, 111; identity, 8, 106, 107

third-plus generation Mexican
Americans, 7, 9, 11, 12, 13, 23, 24;
and assigned identities, 106–7,
115; and Chicano identity, 105;
definition of, 6; demographic
aspects of, 67; and ethnic identity
professional organizations,
58, 59; and intermarriage, 88;
language ability of, 35; and
Mexican ethnicity, 95–96, 100; and
Mexican food, 27, 29; and ongoing
immigration, 112–13; and Spanish-
language television, 40, 42; and
volunteer work, 54
traditional gender roles, 31, 32, 36, 41
Treaty of Guadalupe Hidalgo, 18
Tucson, Arizona, 37, 46

underclass, 97
United Farm Workers Union, 112
United States, 3, 10, 13, 14, 24;
Chicana/o identity and time spent
in, 101; Civil Rights Movement
and, 122; economy of, 7, 92, 112;
intermarriage in, 77–79, 83, 91;
language-based discrimination
in, 36; Latinos in, 40, 54, 61; and
Mexican American population, 72,
109, 117; population of, 29, 70–71,
125; racial categories of, 67–68,
76; social construction of Mexican
ethnicity in, 95, 99, 104–6, 110,
126–33; and structural pluralism, 45
U.S. Census, 5, 10, 68, 69, 100, 127
U.S.–Mexican War, 14
U.S.–Mexico Border, 3, 5, 14, 79, 84, 131
urban setting, 8, 9, 15, 16, 120

Vasconcelos, José, 121
vendido, 35
Vietnam War, 126
Villa, Pancho, 14
voluntary associations, 48, 52, 65, 95,
96, 99, 115
volunteer work, 23, 45, 46, 48–54, 60
Voting Rights Act, 68, 99

wages: working-class, 15, 21, 115
Waters, Mary, 95, 98, 99, 111
Welfare Reform Act, 125
whites, 14, 17; demographic aspects
of, 72, 74; and intermarriage, 83,
91; and official categories of race,
127; and race ideology, 114; and
reverse discrimination, 63, 64; and
workplace, 55–57. *See also* Anglo
Americans
Winant, Howard, 98, 99, 122
workers, 103, 131; farm, 15; seasonal
low-wage, 16; skilled, 6, 97
workforce: adult, 11, 62; professional,
61, 65
working-class neighborhoods, 17, 19,
20, 82, 92, 116
workplace, 10, 45, 52–58, 61, 63, 65, 67;
professional, 44, 50, 131
world exploration, 26
World War II, 9, 17, 18, 19, 34, 76, 122

xenophobia, 16, 20, 45

younger generation, 30, 46

Zapata, Emiliano, 14

About the Author

Thomas Macias completed his Ph.D. in sociology at the University of Wisconsin, Madison, in 2002 and is currently an assistant professor in the Department of Sociology at the University of Vermont in Burlington. An underlying theme in his research is the question of categorical ambiguity. How confident are we that the array of race and ethnic options given in the U.S. census, for example, reflects anything like the lived experience of race and ethnicity? How shall we classify the growing number of children of mixed-race background? What impact do the long-term effects of language assimilation, intermarriage, and social integration have on the persistence of racial and ethnic categories among groups as we now define them? Macias' recent publications include "The Changing Structure of Structural Assimilation: Organizational Participation among Third-plus-Generation Mexican Americans," from the December 2003 issue of *Social Science Quarterly*, and "Imaginandose Mexicano: The Symbolic Context of Mexican American Ethnicity beyond the Second Generation," in the Fall 2004 issue of *Qualitative Sociology*. His current research interests include comparative work examining the similarities and differences between Western European countries currently experiencing large-scale immigration from parts of northern Africa and Eastern Europe, and the United States' contemporary context of immigration from Asia and Latin America.